Modern English Essays

(Volume V)

Ernest Rhys

Alpha Editions

This edition published in 2019

ISBN : 9789353800765

Design and Setting By
Alpha Editions
email - alphaedis@gmail.com

This book is a reproduction of an important historical work. Alpha Editions uses the best technology to reproduce historical work in the same manner it was first published to preserve its original nature. Any marks or number seen are left intentionally to preserve its true form.

MODERN ENGLISH ESSAYS
VOLUME FIVE

A. G. G.
J. C. SQUIRE
J. HUNEKER
C. BAKEWELL
G. SANTAYANA
VIDA SCUDDER
A. CLUTTON-BROCK
EDWARD GARNETT
MAURICE HEWLETT
JOHN GALSWORTHY
J. MIDDLETON MURRY
GEORGE SAMPSON
H. J. MASSINGHAM
EDMOND HOLMES
ALFRED NOYES
ROBERT LYND
W. H. HUDSON
A. C. BENSON
GRACE RHYS
A. A. MILNE
E. RHYS

1922
LONDON & TORONTO
J. M. DENT & SONS LTD.
NEW YORK: E. P. DUTTON & CO.

All rights reserved

PRINTED IN GREAT BRITAIN

EDITOR'S NOTE

IN this volume the short essay holds the field, whether its prevalence be owing to the impatience of the modern reader, to a feeling for concision in the writer, or to the effect of the daily and weekly press and the demand for an essay that is an article. The variety of subject is equalled by the variety of mode: expert, rapid, deliberating, easy-going in turn. There are veterans in the book like the late W. H. Hudson, who was writing almost up to the day of his death. His *Samphire Gatherer* comes from a volume of 1921. There are new essayists like H. J. Massingham, another devoted bird-lover, and writer on wild life. There are two novelists, John Galsworthy and Maurice Hewlett, who have turned occasional essayist. Of stated essayists, no need to say that A. G. Gardiner is "Alpha of the Plough," whose holiday essay comes from *Windfalls*; or that A. C. Benson, whose essay on the art itself is now published for the first time, is the author of a whole cycle of essays; or that Mr. Clutton-Brock has, by his *Times Literary Supplement* articles, shown again how to give the periodical essay the savour of permanent things.

EDITOR'S NOTE

In Edward Garnett we have a literary diviner, a reviewer, an occasional essayist, who is old enough to have welcomed Conrad and W. H. Hudson. His book *Friday Nights* was only published this year. He has written for *The Nation* since the days when it had another name. Robert Lynd's estimate of Hawthorne is from *The New Statesman*; and we are again reminded of *The Athenæum* in its latest reincarnation by the essay on John Clare of J. Middleton Murry, who is its present editor and a critic of insight. The essays by the editor of *The London Mercury*, J. C. Squire, include one written before that miscellany and review had begun. He reminds us that five poets are among the prose-writers in this volume; which is a significant relation between the two modes. Mr. A. A. Milne is not the only playwright, and his droll fantasia " On Going Dry " adds *Punch* to the list of essayists' weeklies. Of the " Everyman " essays included, George Sampson's on Walter Bagehot and Professor Bakewell's on William James ought to be noted. The latter is a professor at Harvard; and two other American writers are represented—Miss Scudder, whose Plato article is from *The Yale Review*, and the late James Huneker, whose essay on Henry James is from *Unicorns*. The final essay on the late W. H. Hudson, from *The Nineteenth Century and After*, was written two years ago. It has been added as this volume went to press, on the news of his death.

E. R.

For the kind permission to use copyright essays in this volume, special acknowledgments are due to:

Mr. A. C. Benson for " The Art of the Essayist."
Mr. Clutton-Brock and Messrs. Methuen for " The Magic Flute " from *Essays on Art*.
Mr. John Galsworthy, Messrs. Heinemann, and Messrs. Scribner for " Reverie of a Sportsman."
Mr. A. G. Gardiner and Messrs. Dutton for " On Taking a Holiday."
Mr. Edward Garnett, Mr. Jonathan Cape, and Mr. Duckworth for " Jefferies' *Amaryllis*."
Mr. Maurice Hewlett and Messrs. Geo. Bell and Sons for " The Crystal Vase."
Mr. Robert Lynd and Mr. Cobden Sanderson for " Hawthorne."
Mr. H. J. Massingham for " The Venice of England."
Mr. A. A. Milne, Messrs. Methuen, and Messrs. Dutton for " On Going Dry."
Mr. J. Middleton Murry, Messrs. Collins, and Messrs. Dutton for " John Clare."
Mrs. Rhys for " The Five Images of Love."
Mr. Santayana for " Heathenism."
Mr. J. C. Squire and Messrs. Hodder and Stoughton for " A Dead Man " and " The Lonely Author."
Mr. Werner Laurie and Messrs. Scribner for the late James Huneker's " Note on Henry James."
Miss Scudder and *The Yale Review* for " Plato as a Novelist."
Mr. Edmond Holmes for " The Spitalfields Weavers."
The Nineteenth Century and After for " A Rare Traveller."

The remaining essays are reprinted from copyright works in Messrs. Dent's own published list, including " Everyman's Library."

CONTENTS

	PAGE
"The Magic Flute" (*A. Clutton-Brock*)	1
Hawthorne (*Robert Lynd*)	10
On Taking a Holiday (*A. G. Gardiner*)	17
Reverie of a Sportsman (*John Galsworthy*)	21
The Samphire Gatherer (*W. H. Hudson*)	35
Heathenism (*G. Santayana*)	41
The Art of the Essayist (*A. C. Benson*)	50
A Note on Henry James (*James Huneker*)	64
A Dead Man (*J. C. Squire*)	77
The Lonely Author (*J. C. Squire*)	82
Walter Bagehot (*George Sampson*)	87
Richard Jefferies' "Amaryllis at the Fair" (*Edward Garnett*)	102
The Poetry of John Clare (*J. Middleton Murry*)	112
On Going Dry (*A. A. Milne*)	128
The Venice of England (*H. J. Massingham*)	133
William Morris (*Alfred Noyes*)	150
William James and his Work (*Charles M. Bakewell*)	164
The Five Images of Love (*Grace Rhys*)	174
The Recreations of the Spitalfields Weavers (*Edmond G. A. Holmes*)	178
The Crystal Vase (*Maurice Hewlett*)	194
Plato as a Novelist (*Vida D. Scudder*)	210
A Rare Traveller: W. H. Hudson (*Ernest Rhys*)	233

MODERN ENGLISH ESSAYS

"THE MAGIC FLUTE"
By A. Clutton-Brock

WHEN *The Magic Flute* was produced by the already dying Mozart it had little success. At the first performance, it is said, when the applause was faint, the leader of the orchestra stole up to Mozart, who was conducting, and kissed his hand; and Mozart stroked him on the head. We may guess that the leader knew what the music meant and that Mozart knew that he knew. Neither could put it into words and it is not put into words in the libretto. But the libretto need not be an obstruction to the meaning of the music if only the audience will not ask themselves what the libretto means. After Mozart's death the opera was successful, no doubt because the audience had given up asking what the libretto meant and had learnt something of the meaning of the music.

There are worse librettos—librettos which have some clear unmusical meaning of their own beyond which the audience cannot penetrate to the meaning of the music, if it has any. This libretto, apart from the music, is so nearly meaningless, it has so little coherence, that one can easily pass through it to the music. The author, Schickaneder, was Mozart's friend, and he had wit enough to understand the mood of Mozart. That mood does express itself in the plot and the incidents of the libretto, although in them it is empty of value or passion. Schickaneder, in fact, constructed a mere diagram to which Mozart gave life. The life is all in the music, but the diagram has its use, in that it supplies a shape, which we recognise, to the life of the music. The characters live in the music, but in the words they tell us something about themselves which enables us to understand their musical speech better. Papageno tells us that he is a bird-catcher and a child of nature. The words are labels, but through them we pass more quickly to an understanding of his song. Only we shall miss that understanding if we try to reach it through the words, if we look for the story of the opera in them. In the words the events of the opera have no connexion with each other. There is no reason why one should follow another. The logic of it is all in the music, for the music creates a world in which events happen naturally, in which one tune springs out of another, or conflicts with it, like the forces of nature or the thoughts and actions of man. This world is the universe as Mozart sees it; and the whole opera is an expression of his peculiar faith.

It is therefore a religious work, though free from that meaningless and timid solemnity which we

"THE MAGIC FLUTE"

associate with religion. Mozart, in this world, was like an angel who could not but laugh, though without any malice, at all the bitter earnestness of mankind. Even the wicked were only absurd to him; they were naughty children whom, if one had the spell, one could enchant into goodness. And in *The Magic Flute* the spell works. It works in the flute itself and in Papageno's lyre when the wicked negro Monostatos threatens him and Tamino with his ugly attendants. Papageno has only to play a beautiful childish tune on his lyre and the attendants all march backwards to an absurd goose-step in time with it. They are played off the stage; and the music convinces one that they must yield to it. So, we feel, if we had had the music, we could have made the Prussians march their goose-step back to Potsdam; so we could play all solemn perversity off the stage of life. If we had the music—but there is solemn perversity in us too; by reason of which we can hardly listen to the music, much less play it, hardly listen to it or understand it even when Mozart makes it for us. For he had the secret of it; he was a philosopher who spoke in music and so simply that the world missed his wisdom and thought that he was just a beggar playing tunes in the street. A generation ago he was commonly said to be too tuney, as you might say that a flower was too flowery. People would no more consider him than they would consider the lilies of the field. They preferred Wagner in all his glory.

A. CLUTTON-BROCK

Even now you can enjoy *The Magic Flute* as a more than usually absurd musical comedy with easy, old-fashioned tunes. You can enjoy it anyway, if you are not solemn about it, as you can enjoy *Hamlet* for a bloody melodrama. But, like *Hamlet*, it has depths and depths of meaning beyond our full comprehension. Papageno is a pantomime figure, but he is also one of the greatest figures in the drama of the world. He is Everyman, like Hamlet, if only we had the wit to recognise ourselves in him. Or rather he is that element in us which we all like and despise in others, but which we will never for one moment confess to in ourselves—the coward, the boaster, the liar, but the child of nature. He, because he knows himself for all of these, can find his home in Sarastro's paradies. He does not want Sarastro's high wisdom; what he does want is a Papagena, an Eve, a child of nature like himself; and she is given to him. He has the wit to recognise his mate, almost a bird like himself, and to them Mozart gives their bird-duet, so that, when they sing it, we feel that we might all sing it together. It is not above our capacity of understanding or delight. The angel has learnt our earthly tongue, but transformed it so that he makes a heaven of the earth, a heaven that is not too high or difficult for us, a wild-wood heaven, half-absurd, in which we can laugh as well as sing, and in which the angels will laugh at us and with us, laugh our silly sorrows into joy.

There is Mozart himself in Papageno, the faun

"THE MAGIC FLUTE"

domesticated and sweetened by centuries of Christian experience, yet still a faun and always ready to play a trick on human solemnity; and in this paradise which Mozart makes for us the faun has his place and a beauty not incongruous with it, like the imps and gargoyles of a Gothic church. At any moment the music will turn from sublimity into fun, and in a moment it can turn back to sublimity; and always the change seems natural. It is like a great cathedral with High Mass and children playing hide-and-seek behind the pillars; and the Mass would not be itself without the children. That is the mind of Mozart which people have called frivolous, just because in his heaven there is room for everything except the vulgar glory of Solomon and cruelty and stupidity and ugliness. There never was anything in art more profound or beautiful than Sarastro's initiation music, but it is not, like the solemnities of the half-serious, incongruous with the twitterings of Papageno. Mozart's religion is so real that it seems to be not religion, but merely beauty, as real saints seem to be not good, but merely charming. And there are people to whom his beauty does not seem to be art, because it is just beauty; they think that he had the trick of it and could turn it on as he chose; they prefer the creaking of effort and egotism. His gifts are so purely gifts and so lavish that they seem to be cheap; and *The Magic Flute* is an absurdity which he wrote in a hurry to please the crowd.

We can hardly expect to see a satisfying performance of it on the stage of to-day, but we must be grateful for any performance, for the life of the music is in it. One can see from it what *The Magic Flute* might be. The music is so sung, so played that it does transfigure the peculiar theatrical hideousness of our time. Tamino and Pamina may look like figures out of an Academy picture, as heroes and heroines of opera always do. They may wear clothes that belong to no world of reality or art, clothes that suggest the posed and dressed-up model. But the music mitigates even these, and it helps every one to act, or rather to forget what they have learnt about acting. It evidently brings happiness and concord to those who sing it, so that they seem to be taking part in a religious act rather than in an act of the theatre. One feels this most in the concerted music, when the same wind from paradise seems to be blowing through all the singers and they move to it like flowers, in spite of their absurd clothes.

But what is needed for a satisfying performance is a world congruous to the eye as well as to the ear; and for this we need a break with all our theatrical conventions. Sarastro, for instance, lives among Egyptian scenery—very likely the architecture of his temple was Egyptian at the first performance—but, for all that, this Egyptian world does not suit the music, and to us it suggests the miracles of the Egyptian Hall. But there is one world which would perfectly suit the music, a world in which it could pass naturally from absurdity

"THE MAGIC FLUTE"

to beauty, and in which all the figures could be harmonious and yet distinct, and that is the Chinese world as we know it in Chinese art. For in that there is something fantastic yet spiritual, something comic but beautiful, a mixture of the childish and the sacred, which might say to the eye what Mozart's music says to the ear. Only in Chinese art could Papageno be a saint; only in that world, which ranges from the willow-pattern plate to the Rishi in his mystical ecstasy in the wilderness, could the soul of Mozart, with its laughter and its wisdom, be at home. That too is the world in which flowers and all animals are of equal import with mankind; it is the world of dragons in which the serpent of the first act would not seem to be made of pasteboard, and in which all the magic would not seem to be mere conjuring. In that world one might have beautiful landscapes and beautiful figures to suit them. There Sarastro would not be a stage magician, but a priest; from Papageno and the lovers to him would be only the change from Ming to Sung, which would seem no change at all. Chinese art, in fact, is the world of the magic flute, the world where silver bells hang on every flowering tree and the thickets are full of enchanted nightingales. It is the world of imps and monsters, and yet of impassioned contemplation, where the sage sits in a moonlit pavilion and smiles like a lover, and where the lovers smile like sages; where everything is to the eye what the music of Mozart is to the ear.

A. CLUTTON-BROCK

In the Chinese world we could be rid of all the drawling erotics of the modern theatre, we could give up the orchid for the lotus and the heavy egotism of Europe for the self-forgetful gaiety of the East. It may be only an ideal world, empty of the horrors of reality, but it is one which the art of China makes real to us and with which we are familiar in that art; and there is a smiling wisdom in it, there is a gaiety which comes from conquest rather than refusal of reality, just like the gaiety and wisdom of Mozart's music. He knew sorrow well, but would not luxuriate in it; he took the beauty of the universe more seriously than himself. To him wickedness was a matter of imps and monsters rather than of villains, and of imps and monsters that could be exorcised by music. He was the Orpheus of the world who might tame the beast in all of us if we would listen to him, the wandering minstrel whom the world left to play out in the street. And yet his ultimate seriousness and the last secret of his beauty is pity, not for himself and his own little troubles, but for the whole bitter earnestness of mortal children. And in this pity he seems not to weep for us, still less for himself, but to tell us to dry our tears and be good, and listen to his magic flute. That is what he would have told the Prussians, after he had set them marching the goose-step backwards. Even they would not be the villains of a tragedy for him, but only beasts to be tamed with his music until they should be fit to sing their own bass part in the last

"THE MAGIC FLUTE"

chorus of reconciliation. And this pity of his sounds all through *The Magic Flute* and gives to its beauty a thrill and a wonder far beyond what any fleshly passion can give. Sarastro is a priest, not a magician, because there is in him the lovely wisdom of pity, because he has a place in his paradise for Papageno, the child of nature, where he shall be made happy with his mate Papagena. There is a moment when Papageno is about to hang himself because there is no one to love him; he will hang himself in Sarastro's lonely paradise. But there is a sly laughter in the music which tells us that he will be interrupted with the rope round his neck. And so he is, and Papagena is given to him, and the paradise is no longer lonely; and the two sing their part in the chorus of reconciliation at the end. And we are sure that the Queen of Night, and the ugly negro and all his goose-stepping attendants, are not punished. They have been naughty for no reason that anyone can discover, just like Prussians and other human beings; and now the magic flute triumphs over their naughtiness, and the silver bells ring from every tree and the enchanted nightingales sing in all the thickets, and the sages and the lovers smile like children; and the laughter passes naturally into the divine beauty of Mozart's religion, which is solemn because laughter and pity are reconciled in it, not rejected as profane.

HAWTHORNE

By Robert Lynd

HAWTHORNE is the only American admitted into the English Men of Letters Series. This may be partly accidental, and due to the fact that it was possible to get so fine a critic as Henry James to write about him. It also suggests, however, that in 1879 Hawthorne was held in higher esteem than he is held to-day. There are several American writers about whom we are nowadays more curious. Emerson does not soar at quite such an altitude as he once did, but he is still an indubitable figure of genius on the sunny side of the clouds. Thoreau, with the challenge of his sardonic simplicity, will interest us so long as there is a society to protest against. Poe, after we have refined him in the fiercest fires of criticism, remains gold of the most precious. Whitman holds us as the giant aborigine of democracy as well as the rhapsodist of brotherhood and death. Washington Irving, on the other hand, has disappeared except from the school-books, and Oliver Wendell Holmes has ceased to be read by people under fifty. Longfellow has become an exiguous contributor to an anthology except in so far as he is taught, like Irving, to schoolchildren, and Lowell is oftener quoted by politicians than by critics of letters. There is no need to discuss just now whether this waning of reputations is likely to be permanent. It is enough to note that Hawthorne, though he has not waned to the extent that Longfellow has, has ceased for most readers to be a star of the first or second magnitude. How many critics would now place him, as he was once placed, among the great masters of English prose? How many editors of a series of lives of great writers would unhesitatingly include in it a life of Nathaniel Hawthorne?

Hawthorne may nevertheless justly be regarded as a classic, and there have been few writers whose short stories would bear re-reading so well as Hawthorne's three-quarters of a century after their first appearance. The prose, as anyone may see by dipping into Mr. Carl van Doren's admirable selection from *Twice-told Tales*, *Mosses from an Old Manse*, and *The Snow Image*, is beautiful prose, even if it falls short of supreme greatness. It flows with a rhythm at once charming and forceful. It is transparent, and through it we can see life as Hawthorne's imagination played on it like sunlight refracted through water. He is a music-maker rather than a phrase-maker in his use of words. Movement is more to him than metaphor, though he can combine them attractively, as in the opening sentence of *The Seven Vagabonds*:

> Rambling on foot in the spring of my life and the summer of the year, I came one afternoon to a point which gave me the choice of three directions.

ROBERT LYND

You may turn Hawthorne's pages almost at random, and you can scarcely help noticing example after example of this characteristic rhythm of his. It is noticeable even in such a simple narrative sentence as that with which *The Artist of the Beautiful* opens :

> An elderly man, with his pretty daughter on his arm, was passing along the street, and emerged from the gloom of the cloudy evening into the light that fell across the pavement from the window of a small shop.

And, again, we find it in a meditative passage ·

> I saw mankind, in this weary old age of the world, either enduring a sluggish existence amid the smoke and dust of cities, or, if they breathed a purer air, still lying down at night with no hope but to wear out to-morrow, and all the to-morrows which make up life, among the same dull scenes and in the same wretched toil that had darkened the sunshine of to-day.

This all flows with something of the noble ease of hexameters, yet without falling into the vices of pseudo-poetic prose. The mere sound of his sentences gives Hawthorne's prose a wonderful momentum that keeps us interested even when at times we begin to wonder if his subject-matter is quite as interesting as it ought to be. This grave and equable momentum is one of his greatest technical qualities. It is a quality that cannot be adequately illustrated in single sentences or detached passages, because its success is not the success of occasional felicities but of something sustained and pervasive. It may even be imputed as a fault to Hawthorne that he can never, or almost never, escape from the equable rhythm of his prose. He seldom ends a story with the slightly different momentum due to an ending. It is not merely, however, that his stories end quietly: he is like a rider who rides beautifully but does not know how to dismount. He maintains his graceful ease of motion until the last moment, and then he slides off as best he can.

But it would be folly to regard Hawthorne's rhythm as wholly—or even mainly—a technical quality. The rhythm of prose is never that, and it is in vain to play the sedulous ape to the great masters if nothing but their style is imitated. It is not an accident that the greatest English prose is to be found in the Bible. The rhythm of the greatest prose seems at times the rhythm of the spirit of man as it contemplates the life of men in the light of eternity. The rhythm of a Plato, a Milton, a Sir Thomas Browne, is inevitably of a kind that a Jane Austen or a Thackeray, with all their genius, could never achieve. It is the echo of the emotion felt by men to whom time and place are fables with another meaning besides that which appears on the surface. The realists can never write the greatest prose, because to them the world they see is not fabulous but a hard fact. The greatest writers all see the world as fabulous. Their men and women are inhabited by angels or devils, or, on a lower plane, have something of the nature of ghosts or fairies or goblins. If Othello were not a fable as well as a man, he would be no better than a criminal lunatic. If King Lear were not a fable as well as a man, he would be a subject for the psycho-analyst. Imagine either of them as a modern Englishman, putting his case before a judge and jury, and you will see how the artist, even though his characters as a rule are characters such as may be found in reality, must remove them out of and above reality into the region of fables in order to make them permanently real to the imagination. Dickens turned Victorian England into a myth peopled by goblins. Dostoievsky turned Russia into a myth peopled by goblins and demons. It is not that they denied the reality of the world before their eyes, but that they saw within it and about it another world apart from which it had very little meaning.

Hawthorne was a writer extremely conscious of this second world within and about the world. He had abandoned the Puritanical orthodoxy of his people, but none the less he was haunted like them by a sense of a second meaning in life beyond the surface meaning of the day's work and the day's play. Many of his stories are stories in which, as in *Young Goodman Brown*, everyday reality passes into fable and back again as swiftly as though the two worlds were but different stages in a transformation scene. His genius turned more naturally to allegory than any other writer's since Bunyan. This is generally counted a defect, and, indeed if, instead of alternating the everyday world with the fabulous world, he had interwoven them in such a way that the world never became less real on account of the fable it bore within it like an inner light, Hawthorne would have been a greater writer. At the same time, it is better that he should have sacrificed observation than that he should have sacrificed imagination. He lived in an atmosphere in which it must have been extraordinarily difficult to stand sufficiently remote from everyday life to see it not merely with the eye but with the imagination. To the eye, there must have been little enough of fantasy in the narrow lives of the men and women about him. "Never comes any bird of Paradise into that dismal region," he wrote of the Custom-house in which he passed so many years and that made "such havoc of his wits." He had to transform his surroundings into a strange land into which a bird of Paradise might enter. He did this by the invention of a sort of moral fairyland, into which he could project his vision of the mystery of human life. He often offends our sense of reality, but he never leaves us in doubt of the reality of this moral fairyland as the image of all he knew and felt about human life. It is a Puritanical fairyland into which sin has come. But, strong though his sense of sin is, Hawthorne does not always in his view of sin agree with the Puritans. He is more Christian, and he condemns the sin of self-righteousness more than the sins of the flesh. Even so, his imagination is very close to that of the Puritans, who believed in witches and in men possessed by the Devil. The difference is that Hawthorne was inclined to believe that the good church-going people were also witches and men possessed by the Devil. Unless I misunderstand *Young Goodman Brown*, Hawthorne is here telling us how he was tempted to believe this, and reproaching himself for having given way to temptation. In *The Scarlet Letter*, the egoism of the vengeful husband, not the adultery of the wife or the cowardice of the minister who sins with her, is the unpardonable sin of the story. That Hawthorne's imaginative morality had the vehemence of genius is shown by the fact that *The Scarlet Letter* still holds us under its spell in days in which moral values have subtly and swiftly changed. People are no longer thrilled at the thought of a scarlet A on a woman's breast; they would scarcely be thrilled by the spectacle of a whole scarlet alphabet hung round a woman's neck like a collar. Yet Hawthorne's novel survives—a fable of the permanent and dubious warfare between good and evil, in which good changes its shape into that of evil, and evil is transmuted into good through suffering. His genius survives, like that of Hans Andersen, because, not only does it carry the burden of morality, but it is led on its travels by a fancy wayward and caressing as the summer wind. He is the first prose myth-maker of America, and he has left no successors in his kind.

ON TAKING A HOLIDAY
By A. G. Gardiner
(" *Alpha of the Plough* ")

I hope the two ladies from the country who have been writing to the newspapers to know what sights they ought to see in London during their Easter holiday will have a nice time. I hope they will enjoy the tube and have fine weather for the Monument, and whisper to each other successfully in the whispering gallery of St. Paul's, and see the dungeons at the Tower and the seats of the mighty at Westminster, and return home with a harvest of joyful memories. But I can promise them that there is one sight they will not see. They will not see me. Their idea of a holiday is London. My idea of a holiday is forgetting there is such a place as London.

Not that I dislike London. I should like to see it. I have long promised myself that I would see it. Some day, I have said, I will surely have a look at this place. It is a shame, I have said, to have lived in it so long and never to have seen it. I suppose I am not much worse than other Londoners. Do you, sir, who have been taking the morning bus from Balham for heaven knows how many years—do you, when you are walking down Fleet Street, stand still with a shock of delight as the dome of St. Paul's and its cross of gold burst on your astonished sight? Do you go on a fine afternoon and take your stand on Waterloo Bridge to see that wondrous river façade that stretches with its cloud-capped towers and gorgeous palaces from Westminster to St. Paul's? Do you know the spot where Charles was executed, or the church where there are the best Grinling Gibbons carvings? Did you ever go into Somerset House to see the will of William Shakespeare, or—in short, did you ever see London? Did you ever see it, not with your eyes merely, but with your mind, with the sense of revelation, of surprise, of discovery? Did you ever see it as those two ladies from the country will see it this Easter as they pass breathlessly from wonder to wonder? Of course not. You need a holiday in London as I do. You need to set out with young Tom (aged ten) on a voyage of discovery and see all the sights of this astonishing city as though you had come to it from a far country.

That is how I hope to visit it—some day. But not this Easter, not when I know the beech woods are dressing themselves in green and the cherry blossoms are out in the orchards and the great blobs of the chestnut tree are ready to burst, and the cuckoo is calling all day long and the April meadows are "smoored wi' new grass," as they say in the Yorkshire dales. Not when I know that by putting down a bit of paper at the magic casement at Paddington I can be whisked between sunset and

ON TAKING A HOLIDAY

dawn to the fringe of Dartmoor and let loose—shall it be from Okehampton or Bovey Tracy or Moreton Hampstead? what matter the gate by which we enter the sanctuary?—let loose, I say, into the vast spaces of earth and sky where the moorland streams sing their ancient runes over the boulders and the great tors stand out like castles of the gods against the horizon and the Easter sun dances, as the legend has it, overhead and founders gloriously in the night beyond Plymouth Sound.

Or, perhaps, ladies, if you come from the North, I may pass you unawares, and just about the time when you are cracking your breakfast egg in the boarding house at Russell Square—heavens, Russell Square!—and discussing whether you shall first go down the deepest lift or up the highest tower, or stand before the august ugliness of Buckingham Palace, or see the largest station or the smallest church, I shall be stepping out from Keswick, by the lapping waters of Derwentwater, hailing the old familiar mountains as they loom into sight, looking down again—think of it!—into the Jaws of Borrowdale, having a snack at Rosthwaite, and then, hey for Styehead! up, up ever the rough mountain track, with the buzzard circling with slow flapping wings about the mountain flanks, with glorious Great Gable for my companion on the right hand and no less glorious Scafell for my companion on the left hand, and at the rocky turn in the track — lo! the great amphitheatre of Wasdale, the last sanctuary of lakeland.

A. G. GARDINER

And at this point, ladies, you may as you crane your neck to see the Duke of York at the top of his column—wondering all the while who the deuce the fellow was that he should stand so high—you may, I say, if you like, conceive me standing at the top of the pass, taking my hat from my head and pronouncing a terrific curse on the vandals who would desecrate the last temple of solitude by driving a road over this fastness of the mountains in order that the gross tribe of motorists may come with their hoots and their odours, their hurry and vulgarity, and chase the spirit of the mountains away from us for ever. . . . And then by the screes of Great Gable to the hollow among the mountains. Or perchance, I may turn by Sprinkling Tarn and see the Pikes of Langdale come into view and stumble down Rossett Ghyll and so by the green pastures of Langdale to Grasmere.

In short, ladies, I may be found in many places. But I shall not tell you where. I am not quite sure that I could tell you where at this moment, for I am like a fellow who has come into great riches and is doubtful how he can squander them most gloriously. But, I repeat, ladies, that you will not find me in London I leave London to you. May you enjoy it.

REVERIE OF A SPORTSMAN

By John Galsworthy

I set out one morning in late August, with some potted grouse sandwiches in one pocket and a magazine in the other, for a tramp toward Causdon. I had not been in that particular part of the moor since I used to go snipe-shooting there as a boy— my first introduction, by the way, to sport. It was a very lovely day, almost too hot; and I never saw the carpet of the moor more exquisite—heather, fern, the silvery white cotton grass, dark peat turves, and green bog-moss, all more than customarily clear in hue under a very blue sky. I walked till two o'clock, then sat down in a little scoop of valley by a thread of stream, which took its rise from an awkward-looking bog at the top. It was wonderfully quiet. A heron rose below me and flapped away; and while I was eating my potted grouse I heard the harsh cheep of a snipe, and caught sight of the twisting bird vanishing against the line of sky above the bog. "That must have been one of the bogs we used to shoot," I thought; and having finished my snack of lunch, I rolled myself a cigarette, opened the magazine, and idly turned its pages. I had no serious intention of reading—the calm and silence were too seductive, but my attention became riveted by an exciting story of some man-eating lions, and I read on till I had followed the adventure to the death of the two ferocious brutes, and found my cigarette actually burning my fingers. Crushing it out against the dampish roots of the heather, I lay back with my eyes fixed on the sky, thinking of nothing.

Suddenly I became conscious that between me and that sky a leash of snipe high up were flighting and twisting and gradually coming lower; I appeared, indeed, to have a sort of attraction for them. They would dash toward each other, seem to exchange ideas, and rush away again, like flies that waltz together for hours in the centre of a room. As they came lower and lower over me I could almost swear I heard them whisper to each other with their long bills, and presently I absolutely caught what they were saying: " Look at him! The ferocious brute! Oh, look at him!"

Amazed at such an extraordinary violation of all the laws of Nature, I began to rub my ears, when I distinctly heard the " Go-back, go-back " of an old cock grouse, and, turning my head cautiously, saw him perched on a heathery knob within twenty yards of where I lay. Now, I knew very well that all efforts to introduce grouse on Dartmoor have been quite unsuccessful, since for some reason connected with the quality of the heather, the nature of the soil, or the over-mild dampness of the air, this king of game birds most

REVERIE OF A SPORTSMAN

unfortunately refuses to become domiciled there; so that I could hardly credit my senses. But suddenly I heard him also: "Look at him! Go back! The ferocious brute! Go back!" He seemed to be speaking to something just below; and there, sure enough, was the first hare I had ever seen out on the full of the moor. I have always thought a hare a jolly beast, and not infrequently felt sorry when I rolled one over; it has a way of crying like a child if not killed outright. I confess then that in hearing it, too, whisper: "Look at him! The ferocious brute! Oh, look at him!" I experienced the sensation that comes over one when one has not been quite fairly treated. Just at that moment, with a warm stirring of the air, there pitched within six yards of me a magnificent old black-cock—the very spit of that splendid fellow I shot last season at Balnagie, whose tail my wife now wears in her hat. He was accompanied by four gray-hens, who, settling in a semi-circle, began at once: "Look at him! Look at him! The ferocious brute! Oh, look at him!" At that moment I say with candour that I regretted the many times I have spared gray-hens with the sportsmanlike desire to encourage their breed.

For several bewildered minutes after that I could not turn my eyes without seeing some bird or other alight close by me: more and more grouse, and black game, pheasants, partridges—not only the excellent English bird, but the very sporting Hungarian variety—and that unsatisfactory red-legged Frenchman which runs any distance rather than get up and give you a decent shot at him. There were woodcock too, those twisting delights of the sportsman's heart, whose tiny wing-feather trophies have always given me a distinct sensation of achievement when pinned in the side of my shooting-cap; wood-pigeons too, very shy and difficult, owing to the thickness of their breast-feathers—and, after all, only coming under the heading "sundry"; wild duck, with their snaky dark heads, that I have shot chiefly in Canada, lurking among rushes in twilight at flighting time —a delightful sport, exciting, as the darkness grows; excellent eating too, with red pepper and sliced oranges in oil! Certain other sundries kept coming also; landrails, a plump, delicious little bird; green and golden plover; even one of those queer little creatures, moorhens, that always amuse one by their quick, quiet movements, plaintive note, and quaint curiosity, though not really, of course, fit to shoot, with their niggling flight and fishy flavour! Ptarmigan, too, a bird I admire very much, but have only once or twice succeeded in bringing down, shy and scarce as it is in Scotland. And, side by side, the alpha and omega of the birds to be shot in these islands, a capercailzie and a quail. I well remember shooting the latter in a turnip-field in Lincolnshire—a scrap of a bird, the only one I ever saw in England. Apart from the pleasurable sensation at its rarity, I recollect feeling that it was almost a mercy to put the little thing out of

REVERIE OF A SPORTSMAN

its loneliness. It ate very well. There, too, was that loon or northern diver that I shot with a rifle off Denman Island as it swam about fifty yards from the shore. Handsome plumage; I still have the mat it made. One bird only seemed to refuse to alight, remaining up there in the sky, and uttering continually that trilling cry which makes it perhaps the most spiritual of all birds that can be eaten—I mean, of course, the curlew. I certainly never shot one. They fly, as a rule, very high and seem to have a more than natural distrust of the human being. This curlew—ah! and a blue rock (I have always despised pigeon-shooting)—were the only two winged creatures that one can shoot for sport in this country that did not come and sit round me.

There must have been, I should say, as many hundred altogether as I have killed in my time—a tremendous number. They sat in a sort of ring, moving their beaks from side to side, just as I have seen penguins doing on the films that explorers bring back from the Antarctic; and all the time repeating to each other those amazing words: "Look at him! The ferocious brute! Oh, look at him!"

Then, to my increased astonishment, I saw behind the circles of the birds a number of other animals besides the hare. At least five kinds of deer—the red, the fallow, the roe, the common deer, whose name I've forgotten, which one finds in Vancouver Island, and the South African springbok, that swarm in from the Karoo at certain seasons, among which I had that happy week once in Namaqualand, shooting them from horseback after a gallop to cut them off—very good eating as camp fare goes, and making nice rugs if you sew their skins together. There, too, was the hyena I missed, probably not altogether; but he got off, to my chagrin—queer-looking brute! Rabbits of course had come—hundreds and hundreds of them. If—like everybody else—I've done such a lot of it, I can't honestly say I've ever cared much for shooting rabbits, though the effect is neat enough when you get them just right and they turn head over heels—and anyway, the prolific little brutes have to be kept down. There, too, actually was my wild ostrich—the one I galloped so hard after, letting off my Winchester at half a mile, only to see him vanish over the horizon. Next him was the bear whose lair I came across at the Nanaimo Lakes. How I did lurk about to get that fellow! And, by Jove! close to him, two cougars. I never got a shot at them, never even saw one of the brutes all the time I was camping in Vancouver Island, where they lie flat along the branches over your head, waiting to get a chance at deer, sheep, dog, pig, or anything handy. But they had come now sure enough, glaring at me with their greenish cats' eyes—powerful-looking creatures! And next them sat a little meerkat—not much larger than a weasel—without its head! Ah yes!—that trial shot, as we trekked out from Rous' farm, and I wanted to try the little new rifle I had borrowed.

REVERIE OF A SPORTSMAN

It was sitting over its hole fully seventy yards from the wagon, quite unconscious of danger. I just took aim and pulled; and there it was, without its head, fallen across its hole. I remember well how pleased our "boys" were. And I too! Not a bad little rifle, that!

Outside the ring of beasts I could see foxes moving, not mixing with the stationary creatures, as if afraid of suggesting that I had shot them, instead of being present at their deaths in the proper fashion. One, quite a cub, kept limping round on three legs—the one, no doubt, whose pad was given me, out cubbing, as a boy. I put that wretched pad in my hat-box, and forgot it, so that I was compelled to throw the whole stinking show away. There was quite a lot of grown foxes; it certainly showed delicacy on their part, not sitting down with the others. There was really a tremendous crowd of creatures altogether by this time! I should think every beast and bird I ever shot, or even had a chance of killing, must have been there, and all whispering: "Look at him! The ferocious brute! Oh, look at him!"

Animal lover, as every true sportsman is, those words hurt me. If there is one thing on which we sportsmen pride ourselves, and legitimately, it is a humane feeling toward all furred and feathered creatures—and, as every one knows, we are foremost in all efforts to diminish their unnecessary sufferings.

The corroboree about me which they were

obviously holding became, as I grew used to their manner of talking, increasingly audible. But it was the quail's words that I first distinguished.

"He certainly ate me," he said; "said I was good, too!"

"I do not believe"—this was the first hare speaking—"that he shot me for that reason; he did shoot me, and I was jugged, but he wouldn't touch me. And the same day he shot eleven brace of partridges, didn't he?" Twenty-two partridges assented. "And he only ate two of you all told—that proves he didn't want us for food."

The hare's words had given me relief, for I somehow disliked intensely the gluttonous notion conveyed by the quail that I shot merely in order to devour the result. Any one with the faintest instincts of a sportsman will bear me out in this.

When the hare had spoken there was a murmur all round. I could not at first make out its significance, till I heard one of the cougars say: "We kill only when we want to eat"; and the bear, who, I noticed, was a lady, added: "No bear kills anything she cannot devour"; and, quite clear, I caught the quacking words of a wild duck: "We eat every worm we catch, and we'd eat more if we could get them."

Then again from the whole throng came that shivering whisper: "Look at him! The ferocious brute! Oh, look at him!"

In spite of their numbers, they seemed afraid of me, seemed actually to hold me in a kind of

REVERIE OF A SPORTSMAN

horror—me, an animal lover, and without a gun! I felt it bitterly. "How is it," I thought, "that not one of them seems to have an inkling of what it means to be a sportsman, not one of them seems to comprehend the instinct which makes one love sport just for the—er—danger of it?" The hare spoke again.

"Foxes," it murmured, "kill for the love of killing. Man is a kind of fox." A violent dissent at once rose from the foxes, till one of them, who seemed the eldest, said: "We certainly kill as much as we can, but we should always carry it all off and eat it if man gave us time—the ferocious brutes!" You cannot expect much of foxes, but it struck me as especially foxy that he should put the wanton character of his destructiveness off on man, especially when he must have known how carefully we preserve the fox, in the best interests of sport. A pheasant ejaculated shrilly: "He killed sixty of us one day to his own gun, and went off that same evening without eating even a wing!" And again came the shivering whisper: "Look at him! The ferocious brute! Oh, look at him!" It was too absurd! As if they could not realise that a sportsman shoots almost entirely for the mouths of others! But I checked myself, remembering that altruism is a purely human attribute. "They get a big price for us!" said a woodcock, "especially if they shoot us early. *I* fetched several shillings." Really, the ignorance of these birds! As if modern sportsmen knew anything of what happens after a day's shooting! All that is left to the butler and the keeper. Beaters, of course, and cartridges must be paid for, to say nothing of the sin of waste. "I would not think them so much worse than foxes," said a rabbit, "if they didn't often hurt you, so that you take hours dying. I was seven hours dying in great agony, and one of my brothers was twelve. Weren't you, brother?" A second rabbit nodded. "But perhaps that's better than trapping," he said. "Remember mother!" "Ah!" a partridge muttered, "foxes at all events do bite your head off clean. But men often break your wing, or your leg, and leave you!" And again that shivering whisper rose: "Look at him! The ferocious brute! Oh, look at him!"

By this time the whole thing was so getting on my nerves that if I could have risen I should have rushed at them, but a weight as of lead seemed to bind me to the ground, and all I could do was to thank God that they did not seem to know of my condition, for, though there were no man-eaters among them, I could not tell what they might do if they realised that I was helpless—the sentiments of chivalry and generosity being confined to man, as we all know.

"Yes," said the capercailzie slowly, "I am a shy bird, and was often shot at before this one got me; and though I'm strong, my size is so against me that I always took a pellet or two away with me; and what can you do then? Those ferocious brutes take the shot out of their faces and hands

REVERIE OF A SPORTSMAN

when they shoot each other by mistake—I've seen 'em; but we have no chance to do that." A snipe said shrilly: "What I object to is that he doesn't eat us till he's had too much already. I come in on toast at the fifth course; it hurts one's feelings."

"Ferocious brute, killing everything he sees."

I felt my blood fairly boil, and longed to cry out: "You beasts! You know that we don't kill everything we see! We leave that to cockneys, and foreigners." But just as I had no power of movement, so I seemed to have no power of speech. And suddenly a little voice, high up over me, piped down: "They never shoot us larks." I have always loved the lark; how grateful I felt to that little creature—till it added: "They do worse; they take and shut us up in little traps of wire till we pine away! Ferocious brutes!" In all my life I think I never was more disappointed! The second cougar spoke: "He once passed within spring of me. What do you say, friends; shall we go for him?" The shivering answer came from all: "Go for him! Ferocious brute! Oh, go for him!" And I heard the sound of hundreds of soft wings and pads ruffling and shuffling. And, knowing that I had no power to move an inch, I shut my eyes. Lying there motionless, as a beetle that shams dead, I felt them creeping, creeping, till all round me and over me was the sound of nostrils sniffing; and every second I expected to feel the nip of teeth and beaks in the fleshy parts of me. But nothing came, and with an effort I reopened my eyes. There they were, hideously close, with an expression on their faces that I could not read; a sort of wry look, every nose and beak turned a little to one side. And suddenly I heard the old fox saying: "It's impossible, with a smell like that; we could never eat him!" From every one of them came a sort of sniff or sneeze as of disgust, and as they began to back away I distinctly heard the hyena mutter: "He's not wholesome—not wholesome—the ferocious brute!"

The relief of that moment was swamped by my natural indignation that these impudent birds and beasts should presume to think that I, a British sportsman, would not be good to eat. Then that beastly hyena added: If we killed him, you know, and buried him for a few days, he might be tolerable."

An old cock grouse called out at once: "Go back! Let us hang him! *We* are always well hung. They like us a little decayed—ferocious brutes! Go back!" And once more I felt, from the stir and shuffle, that my fate hung in the balance; and I shut my eyes again, lest they might be tempted to begin on them. Then, to my infinite relief, I heard the cougar—have we not always been told that they were the friends of man?—mutter: "Pah! It's clear we could never eat him fresh, and what we do not eat at once we do not touch!"

All the birds cried out in chorus: "No! That would be crow's work." And again I felt that I was saved. Then, to my horror, that infernal loon shrieked: "Kill him and have him stuffed—

specimen of Ferocious Brute! Or fix his skin on a tree, and look at it—as he did with me!"

For a full minute I could feel the currents of opinion swaying over me, at this infamous proposal; then the old black-cock, the one whose tail is in my wife's hat, said sharply: "Specimen! He's not good enough!" And once more, for all my indignation at that gratuitous insult, I breathed freely.

"Come!" said the lady bear quietly: "Let us dribble on him a little, and go. The ferocious brute is not worth more!" And, during what seemed to me an eternity, one by one they came up, deposited on me a little saliva, looking into my eyes the while with a sort of horror and contempt, then vanished on the moor. The last to come up was the little meerkat without its head. It stood there; it could neither look at me nor drop saliva, but somehow it contrived to say: "I forgive you, ferocious brute; but I was very happy!" Then it, too, withdrew. And from all around, out of invisible presences in the air and the heather, came once more the shivering whisper: "Look at him! The ferocious brute! Oh, look at him!"

I sat up. There was a trilling sound in my ears. Above me in the blue a curlew was passing, uttering its cry. Ah! Thank Heaven!—I had been asleep! My day-dream had been caused by the potted grouse, and the pressure of the Review, which had lain, face downwards, on my chest, open at the page where I had been reading about the man-eating lions, and the death of those ferocious brutes. It shows what tricks of disproportion little things will play with the mind when it is not under reasonable control.

And, to get the unwholesome taste of it all out of my mouth, I at once jumped up and started for home at a round pace.

THE SAMPHIRE GATHERER
By W. H. Hudson

At sunset, when the strong wind from the sea was beginning to feel cold, I stood on the top of the sandhill looking down at an old woman hurrying about over the low damp ground beneath—a bit of sea-flat divided from the sea by the ridge of sand; and I wondered at her, because her figure was that of a feeble old woman, yet she moved—I had almost said flitted—over that damp level ground in a surprisingly swift light manner, pausing at intervals to stoop and gather something from the surface. But I couldn't see her distinctly enough to satisfy myself: the sun was sinking below the horizon, and that dimness in the air and coldness in the wind at day's decline, when the year too was declining, made all objects look dim. Going down to her I found that she was old, with thin grey hair on an uncovered head, a lean dark face with regular features and grey eyes that were not old and looked steadily at mine, affecting me with a sudden mysterious sadness. For they were unsmiling eyes and themselves expressed an unutterable sadness, as it appeared to me at the first swift glance; or perhaps not that, as it presently seemed, but a shadowy something which sadness had left in them, when all pleasure and all interest in life forsook her, with all affections, and she no longer cherished either memories or hopes. This may be nothing but conjecture or fancy, but if she had been a visitor from another world she could not have seemed more strange to me.

I asked her what she was doing there so late in the day, and she answered in a quiet even voice which had a shadow in it too, that she was gathering samphire of that kind which grows on the flat saltings and has a dull green leek-like fleshy leaf. At this season, she informed me, it was fit for gathering to pickle and put by for use during the year. She carried a pail to put it in, and a table-knife in her hand to dig the plants up by the roots, and she also had an old sack in which she put every dry stick and chip of wood she came across. She added that she had gathered samphire at this same spot every August end for very many years.

I prolonged the conversation, questioning her and listening with affected interest to her mechanical answers, while trying to fathom those unsmiling, unearthly eyes that looked so steadily at mine.

And presently, as we talked, a babble of human voices reached our ears, and half turning we saw the crowd, or rather procession, of golfers coming from the golf-house by the links where they had been drinking tea. Ladies and gentlemen players, forty or more of them, following in a loose line, in couples and small groups, on their way to the

THE SAMPHIRE GATHERER

Golfers' Hotel, a little further up the coast; a remarkably good-looking lot with well-fed happy faces, well dressed and in a merry mood, all freely talking and laughing. Some were staying at the hotel, and for the others a score or so of motor-cars were standing before its gates to take them inland to their homes, or to houses where they were staying.

We suspended the conversation while they were passing us, within three yards of where we stood, and as they passed the story of the links where they had been amusing themselves since luncheon-time came into my mind. The land there was owned by an old, an ancient, family; they had occupied it, so it is said, since the Conquest; but the head of the house was now poor, having no house property in London, no coal mines in Wales, no income from any other source than the land, the twenty or thirty thousand acres let for farming. Even so he would not have been poor, strictly speaking, but for the sons, who preferred a life of pleasure in town, where they probably had private establishments of their own. At all events they kept race-horses, and had their cars, and lived in the best clubs, and year by year the patient old father was called upon to discharge their debts of honour. It was a painful position for so estimable a man to be placed in, and he was much pitied by his friends and neighbours, who regarded him as a worthy representative of the best and oldest family in the county. But he was compelled to do what he could to make both ends meet, and one of the little things he did was to establish golf-links over a mile or so of sand-hills, lying between the ancient coast village and the sea, and to build and run a Golfers' Hotel in order to attract visitors from all parts. In this way, incidentally, the villagers were cut off from their old direct way to the sea and deprived of those barren dunes, which were their open space and recreation ground and had stood them in the place of a common for long centuries. They were warned off and told that they must use a path to the beach which took them over half a mile from the village. And they had been very humble and obedient and had made no complaint. Indeed, the agent had assured them that they had every reason to be grateful to the overlord, since in return for that trivial inconvenience they had been put to they would have the golfers there, and there would be employment for some of the village boys as caddies. Nevertheless, I had discovered that they were not grateful but considered that an injustice had been done to them, and it rankled in their hearts.

I remembered all this while the golfers were streaming by, and wondered if this poor woman did not, like her fellow-villagers, cherish a secret bitterness against those who had deprived them of the use of the dunes where for generations they had been accustomed to walk or sit or lie on the loose yellow sands among the barren grasses, and had also cut off their direct way to the sea where they went daily in search of bits of firewood and

THE SAMPHIRE GATHERER

whatever else the waves threw up which would be a help to them in their poor lives.

If it be so, I thought, some change will surely come into those unchanging eyes at the sight of all these merry, happy golfers on their way to their hotel and their cars and luxurious homes.

But though I watched her face closely there was no change, no faintest trace of ill-feeling or feeling of any kind; only that same shadow which had been there was there still, and her fixed eyes were like those of a captive bird or animal, that gaze at us, yet seem not to see us but to look through and beyond us. And it was the same when they had all gone by and we finished our talk and I put money in her hand; she thanked me without a smile, in the same quiet even tone of voice in which she had replied to my question about the samphire.

I went up once more to the top of the ridge, and looking down saw her again as I had seen her at first, only dimmer, swiftly, lightly moving or flitting moth-like or ghost-like over the low flat salting, still gathering samphire in the cold wind, and the thought that came to me was that I was looking at and had been interviewing a being that was very like a ghost, or in any case a soul, something which could not be described, like certain atmospheric effects in earth and water and sky which are ignored by the landscape painter. To protect himself he cultivates what is called the "sloth of the eye": he thrusts his fingers into his ears, so to speak, not to hear that mocking voice that follows and mocks him with his miserable limitations. He who seeks to convey his impressions with a pen is almost as badly off: the most he can do in such instances as the one related, is to endeavour to convey the emotion evoked by what he has witnessed.

Let me then take the case of the man who has trained his eyes, or rather whose vision has unconsciously trained itself, to look at every face he meets, to find in most cases something, however little, of the person's inner life. Such a man could hardly walk the length of the Strand and Fleet Street or of Oxford Street without being startled at the sight of a face which haunts him with its tragedy, its mystery, the strange things it has half revealed. But it does not haunt him long; another arresting face follows, and then another, and the impressions all fade and vanish from the memory in a little while. But from time to time, at long intervals, once perhaps in a lustrum, he will encounter a face that will not cease to haunt him, whose vivid impression will not fade for years. It was a face and eyes of that kind which I met in the samphire gatherer on that cold evening; but the mystery of it is a mystery still.

HEATHENISM
By George Santayana

Schopenhauer somewhere observes that the word heathen, no longer in reputable use elsewhere, had found a last asylum in Oxford, the paradise of dead philosophies. Even Oxford, I believe, has now abandoned it; yet it is a good word. It conveys, as no other word can, the sense of vast multitudes tossing in darkness, harassed by demons of their own choice. No doubt it implies also a certain sanctimony in the superior person who uses it, as if he at least were not chattering in the general Babel. What justified Jews, Christians, and Moslems (as Mohammed in particular insisted) in feeling this superiority was the possession of a Book, a chart of life, as it were, in which the most important features of history and morals were mapped out for the guidance of teachable men. The heathen, on the contrary, were abandoned to their own devices, and even prided themselves on following only their spontaneous will, their habit, presumption, or caprice.

Most unprejudiced people would now agree that the value of those sacred histories and rules of life did not depend on their alleged miraculous origin, but rather on that solidity and perspicacity in their authors which enabled them to perceive the laws of sweet and profitable conduct in this world. It was not religion merely that was concerned, at least not that outlying, private, and almost negligible sphere to which we often apply this name; it was the whole fund of experience mankind had gathered by living; it was wisdom. Now, to record these lessons of experience, the Greeks and Romans also had their Books; their history, poetry, science, and civil law. So that while the theologically heathen may be those who have no Bible, the morally and essentially heathen are those who possess no authoritative wisdom, or reject the authority of what wisdom they have; the untaught or unteachable who disdain not only revelation but what revelation stood for among early peoples, namely, funded experience.

In this sense the Greeks were the least heathen of men. They were singularly docile to political experiment, to law, to methodical art, to the proved limitations and resources of mortal life. This life they found closely hedged about by sky, earth, and sea, by war, madness, and conscience with their indwelling deities, by oracles and local genii with their accustomed cults, by a pervasive fate, and the jealousy of invisible gods. Yet they saw that these divine forces were constant, and that they exercised their pressure and bounty with so much method that a prudent art and religion could be built up in their midst. All this was simply a poetic prologue to science and the arts; it largely passed into them,

HEATHENISM

and would have passed into them altogether if the naturalistic genius of Greece had not been crossed in Socrates by a premature discouragement, and diverted into other channels.

Early Hebraism itself had hardly been so wise. It had regarded its tribal and moral interests as absolute, and the Creator as the champion and omnipotent agent of Israel. But this arrogance and inexperience were heathen. Soon the ascendency of Israel over nature and history was proclaimed to be conditional on their fidelity to the Law; and as the spirit of the nation under chastisement became more and more penitential, it was absorbed increasingly in the praise of wisdom. Salvation was to come only by repentance, by being born again with a will wholly transformed and broken; so that the later Jewish religion went almost as far as Platonism or Christianity in the direction opposite to heathenism.

This movement in the direction of an orthodox wisdom was regarded as a progress in those latter days of antiquity when it occurred, and it continued to be so regarded in Christendom until the rise of romanticism. The most radical reformers simply urged that the current orthodoxy, religious or scientific, was itself imperfectly orthodox, being currupt, overloaded, too vague, or too narrow. As every actual orthodoxy is avowedly incomplete and partly ambiguous, a sympathetic reform of it is always in order. Yet very often the reformers are deceived. What really offends them may not be what is false in the received orthodoxy, but what though true is uncongenial to them. In that case heathenism, under the guise of a search for a purer wisdom, is working in their souls against wisdom of any sort. Such is the suspicion that Catholics would throw on Protestantism, naturalists on idealism, and conservatives generally on all revolutions.

But if ever heathenism needed to pose as constructive reform, it is now quite willing and able to throw off the mask. Desire for any orthodox wisdom at all may be repudiated; it may be set down to low vitality and failure of nerve. In various directions at once we see to-day an intense hatred and disbelief gathering head against the very notion of a cosmos to be discovered, or a stable human nature to be respected. Nature, we are told, is an artificial symbol employed by life; truth is a temporary convention; art is an expression of personality; war is better than peace, effort than achievement, and feeling than intelligence; change is deeper than form; will is above morality. Expressions of this kind are sometimes wanton and only half thought out; but they go very deep in the subjective direction. Behind them all is a sincere revulsion against the difficult and confused undertakings of reason; against science, institutions, and moral compulsions. They mark an honest retreat into immediate experience and animal faith. Man used to be called a rational animal, but his rationality is something eventual and ideal, whereas his animality is actual and profound. Heathenism, if we consider life at large, is the primal and universal religion.

It has never been my good fortune to see wild beasts in the jungle, but I have sometimes watched a wild bull in the ring, and I can imagine no more striking, simple, and heroic example of animal faith; especially when the bull is what is technically called noble, that is, when he follows the lure again and again with eternal singleness of thought, eternal courage, and no suspicion of a hidden agency that is mocking him. What the red rag is to this brave creature, their passions, inclinations, and chance notions are to the heathen. What they will they will; and they would deem it weakness and disloyalty to ask whether it is worth willing or whether it is attainable. The bull, magnificently sniffing the air, surveys the arena with the cool contempt and disbelief of the idealist, as if he said: " You seem, you are a seeming; I do not quarrel with you, I do not fear you. I am real, you are nothing." Then suddenly, when his eye is caught by some bright cloak displayed before him, his whole soul changes. His will awakes and he seems to say: " You are my destiny; I want you, I hate you, you shall be mine, you shall not stand in my path. I will gore you. I will disprove you. I will pass beyond you. I shall be, you shall not have been." Later, when sorely wounded and near his end, he grows blind to all these excitements. He smells the moist earth, and turns to the dungeon where an hour ago he was at peace. He remembers the herd, the pasture beyond, and he dreams: "I shall not die, for I love life. I shall be young again, young always, for I love youth. All this outcry is nought to me, this strange suffering is nought. I will go to the fields again, to graze, to roam, to love."

So exactly, with not one least concession to the unsuspected reality, the heathen soul stands bravely before a painted world, covets some bauble, and defies death. Heathenism is the religion of will, the faith which life has in itself because it is life, and in its aims because it is pursuing them.

In their tentative, many-sided, indomitable way, the Germans have been groping for four hundred years towards a restoration of their primitive heathenism. Germany under the long tutelage of Rome had been like a spirited and poetic child brought up by very old and very worldly foster-parents. For many years the elfin creature may drink in their gossip and their maxims with simple wonder; but at last he will begin to be restive under them, ask himself ominous questions, protest, suffer, and finally break into open rebellion. Naturally he will not find at first theories and precepts of his own to take the place of his whole education; he will do what he can with his traditions, revising, interpreting, and patching them with new ideas; and only if he has great earnestness and speculative power will he ever reach an unalloyed expression of his oppressed soul.

Now in Germany speculative power and earnestness existed in a high degree, not, of course, in most

HEATHENISM

people, but in the best and most representative; and it was this *élite* that made the Reformation, and carried it on into historical criticism and transcendental philosophy, until in the nineteenth century, in Schopenhauer, Wagner, and Nietzsche, the last remnants of Christian education were discarded and the spontaneous heathen morality of the race reasserted itself in its purity. That this assertion was not consistent, that it was thrown into the language and images of some alien system, is not to be wondered at; but the Christianity of Parsifal, like the Buddhism of the denial of the will, is a pure piece of romanticism, an exotic setting for those vacillations and sinkings which absolute Will may very well be subject to in its absolute chaos.

The rebellion of the heathen soul is unmistakable in the Reformation, but it is not recognised in this simple form, because those who feel that it was justified do not dream that it was heathen, and those who see that it was heathen will not admit that it was justified. Externally, of course, it was an effort to recover the original essence of Christianity; but why should a free and absolute being care for that original essence when he has discovered it, unless his own mind demanded that very thing? And if his mind demanded it, what need has he to read that demand into an ancient revelation which, as a matter of fact, turned on quite other matters? It was simply the inertia of established prejudice that made people use tradition to correct tradition; until the whole substance of tradition, worn away by that internal friction, should be dissolved, and impulse and native genius should assert themselves unimpeded.

Judaism and Christianity, like Greek philosophy, were singly inspired by the pursuit of happiness, in whatever form it might be really attainable: now on earth if possible, or in the millennium, or in some abstracted and inward life, like that of the Stoics, or in the last resort, in a different life altogether beyond the grave. But heathenism ignores happiness, despises it, or thinks it impossible. The regimen and philosophy of Germany are inspired by this contempt for happiness, for one's own happiness as well as for other people's. Happiness seems to the German moralists something unheroic, an abdication before external things, a victory of the senses over the will. They think the pursuit of happiness low, materialistic, and selfish. They wish everybody to sacrifice or rather to forget happiness, and to do " deeds."

It is in the nature of things that those who are incapable of happiness should have no idea of it. Happiness is not for wild animals, who can only oscillate between apathy and passion. To be happy, even to conceive happiness, you must be reasonable or (if Nietzsche prefers the word) you must be tamed. You must have taken the measure of your powers, tasted the fruits of your passions and learned your place in the world and what things in it can really serve you. To be happy you must be wise. This happiness is sometimes found instinctively,

HEATHENISM

and then the rudest fanatic can hardly fail to see how lovely it is; but sometimes it comes of having learned something by experience (which empirical people never do) and involves some chastening and renunciation; but it is not less sweet for having this touch of holiness about it, and the spirit of it is healthy and beneficent. The nature of happiness, therefore, dawns upon philosophers when their wisdom begins to report the lessons of experience: an *a priori* philosophy can have no inkling of it.

Happiness is the union of vitality with art, and in so far as vitality is a spiritual thing and not mere restlessness and vehemence, art increases vitality. It obviates friction, waste, and despair. Without art, vitality is painful and big with monsters. It is hurried easily into folly and crime; it ignores the external forces and interests which it touches. German philosophy does this theoretically, by dethroning the natural world and calling it an idea created by the ego for its own purposes; and it does this practically also by obeying the categorical imperative—no longer the fabled imperatives of Sinai or of Königsberg, but the inward and vital imperative which the bull obeys, when trusting absolutely in his own strength, rage, and courage, he follows a little red rag and his destiny this way and that way.

THE ART OF THE ESSAYIST

By Arthur Christopher Benson

There is a pleasant story of an itinerant sign-painter who in going his rounds came to a village inn upon whose sign-board he had had his eye for some months and had watched with increasing hope and delight its rapid progress to blurred and faded dimness. To his horror he found a brand-new varnished sign. He surveyed it with disgust, and said to the inn-keeper, who stood nervously by hoping for a professional compliment, "This looks as if someone had been doing it himself."

That sentence holds within it the key to the whole mystery of essay-writing. An essay is a thing which someone does himself; and the point of the essay is not the subject, for any subject will suffice, but the charm of personality. It must concern itself with something "jolly," as the schoolboy says, something smelt, heard, seen, perceived, invented, thought; but the essential thing is that the writer shall have formed his own impression, and that it shall have taken shape in his own mind; and the charm of the essay depends upon the charm of the mind that has conceived and recorded the impression. It will be seen, then, that the essay need not concern itself with anything definite; it need not have an intellectual or a philosophical or a religious or a humorous motif; but equally none of these subjects are ruled out. The only thing necessary is that the thing or the thought should be vividly apprehended, enjoyed, felt to be beautiful, and expressed with a certain gusto. It need conform to no particular rules. All literature answers to something in life, some habitual form of human expression. The stage imitates life, calling in the services of the eye and the ear; there is the narrative of the teller of tales or the minstrel; the song, the letter, the talk—all forms of human expression and communication have their antitypes in literature. The essay is the reverie, the frame of mind in which a man says, in the words of the old song, "Says I to myself, says I."

It is generally supposed that Montaigne is the first writer who wrote what may technically be called essays. His pieces are partly autobiographical, partly speculative, and to a great extent ethical. But the roots of his writing lie far back in literary history. He owed a great part of his inspiration to Cicero, who treated of abstract topics in a conversational way with a romantic background; and this he owed to Plato, whose dialogues undoubtedly contain the germ of both the novel and the essay. Plato is in truth far more the forerunner of the novelist than of the philosopher. He made a background of life, he peopled his scenes with bright boys and amiable elders—oh that all scenes were so peopled!—and he discussed ethical and speculative problems of life and character with a vital rather than with a philosophical interest. Plato's dialogues would be essays but for the fact that they have a dramatic colouring, while the essence of the essay is soliloquy. But in the writings of Cicero, such as the *De Senectute*, the dramatic interest is but slight, and the whole thing approaches far more nearly to the essay than to the novel. Probably Cicero supplied to his readers the function both of the essayist and the preacher, and fed the needs of so-called thoughtful readers by dallying, in a fashion which it is hardly unjust to call twaddling, with familiar ethical problems of conduct and character. The charm of Montaigne is the charm of personality—frankness, gusto, acute observation, lively acquaintance with men and manners. He is ashamed of recording nothing that interested him; and a certain discreet shamelessness must always be the characteristic of the essayist, for the essence of his art is to say what has pleased him without too prudently considering whether it is worthy of the attention of the well-informed mind.

I doubt if the English temperament is wholly favourable to the development of the essayist. In the first place, an Anglo-Saxon likes doing things better than thinking about them; and in his memories, he is apt to recall how a thing was done rather than why it was done. In the next place, we are naturally rather prudent and secretive; we say that a man must not wear his heart upon his sleeve, and that is just what the essayist must do. We have a horror of giving ourselves away, and we like to keep ourselves to ourselves. "The Englishman's home is his castle," says another proverb. But the essayist must not have a castle, or if he does, both the grounds and the living-rooms must be open to the inspection of the public.

Lord Brougham, who revelled in advertisement, used to allow his house to be seen by visitors, and the butler had orders that if a party of people came to see the house, Lord Brougham was to be informed of the fact. He used to hurry to the library and take up a book, in order that the tourists might nudge each other and say in whispers, "There is the Lord Chancellor." That is the right frame of mind for the essayist. He may enjoy privacy, but he is no less delighted that people should see him enjoying it.

The essay has taken very various forms in England. Sir Thomas Browne, in such books as *Religio Medici* and *Urn-Burial*, wrote essays of an elaborate rhetorical style, the long fine sentences winding themselves out in delicate weft-like trails of smoke on a still air, hanging in translucent veils. Addison, in the *Spectator*, treated with delicate humour of life and its problems, and created what was practically a new form in the essay of emotional sentiment evoked by solemn scenes and fine associations. Charles Lamb treated romantically the homeliest stuff of life, and showed how the simplest and commonest experiences were rich in emotion and humour. The beauty and dignity of common life were his theme. De Quincey wrote what may be called impassioned autobiography, and brought to his task a magical control of long-drawn and musical cadences. And then we come to such a writer as Pater, who used the essay for the expression of exquisite artistic sensation. These are only a few instances of the way in which the essay has been used in English literature. But the essence is throughout the same; it is personal sensation, personal impression, evoked by something strange or beautiful or curious or interesting or amusing. It has thus a good deal in common with the art of the lyrical poet and the writer of sonnets, but it has all the freedom of prose, its more extended range, its use of less strictly poetical effects, such as humour in particular. Humour is alien to poetical effect, because poetry demands a certain sacredness and solemnity of mood. The poet is emotional in a reverential way; he is thrilled, he loves, he worships, he sorrows; but it is all essentially grave, because he wishes to recognise the sublime and uplifted elements of life; he wishes to free himself from all discordant, absurd, fantastic, undignified contrasts, as he would extrude laughter and chatter and comfortable ease from some stately act of ceremonial worship. It is quite true that the essayist has a full right to such a mood if he chooses; and such essays as Pater's are all conceived in a sort of rapture of holiness, in a region from which all that is common and homely is carefully fenced out. But

THE ART OF THE ESSAYIST

the essayist may have a larger range, and the strength of a writer like Charles Lamb is that he condescends to use the very commonest materials, and transfigures the simplest experiences with a fairy-like delicacy and a romantic glow. A poet who has far more in common with the range of the essayist is Robert Browning, and there are many of his poems, though not perhaps his best, where his frank amassing of grotesque detail, his desire to include rather than exclude the homelier sorts of emotion, his robust and not very humorous humour, make him an impressionist rather than a lyrist. As literature develops, the distinction between poetry and prose will no doubt become harder to maintain. Coleridge said in a very fruitful maxim: " The opposite of poetry is not prose but science; the opposite of prose is not poetry but verse." That is to say, poetry has as its object the kindling of emotion, and science is its opposite, because science is the dispassionate statement of fact; but prose can equally be used as a vehicle for the kindling of emotion, and therefore may be in its essence poetical: but when it is a technical description of a certain kind of structure its opposite is verse—that is to say, language arranged in metrical and rhythmical form. We shall probably come to think that the essayist is more of a poet than the writer of epics, and that the divisions of literature will tend to be on the one hand the art of clear and logical statement, and on the other the art of emotional and imaginative expression.

ARTHUR CHRISTOPHER BENSON

We must remember in all this that the nomenclature of literature, the attempt to classify the forms of literary expression, is a confusing and a bewildering thing unless it is used merely for convenience. It is the merest pedantry to say that literature must conform to established usages and types. The essence of it is that it is a large force flowing in any channel that it can, and the classification of art is a mere classification of channels. What lies behind all art is the principle of wonder and of arrested attention. It need not be only the sense of beauty; it may be the sense of fitness, of strangeness, of completeness, of effective effort. The amazement of the savage at the sight of a civilised town is not the sense of beauty, it is the sense of force, of mysterious resources, of incredible products, of things unintelligibly and even magically made; and then too there is the instinct for perceiving all that is grotesque, absurd, amusing and jocose, which one sees exhibited in children at the sight of the parrot's crafty and solemn eye and his exaggerated imitation of human speech, at the unusual dress and demeanour of the clown, at the grotesque simulation by the gnarled and contorted tree of something human or reptile. And then, too, there is the strange property in human beings which makes disaster amusing, if its effects are not prejudicial to oneself; that sense which makes the waiter on the pantomime stage, who falls headlong with a tray of crockery, an object to provoke the loudest and most spontaneous mirth of which the ordinary

THE ART OF THE ESSAYIST

human being is capable. The moralist who would be sympathetically shocked at the rueful abrasions of the waiter, or mournful over the waste of human skill and endeavour involved in the breakage, would be felt by all human beings to have something priggish in his compostion and to be too good, as they say, to live.

It is with these rudimentary and inexplicable emotions that the essayist may concern himself, even though the poet be forbidden to do so; and the appeal of the essayist to the world at large will depend upon the extent to which he experiences some common emotion, sees it in all its bearings, catches the salient features of the scene, and records it in vivid and impressive speech.

The essayist is therefore to a certain extent bound to be a spectator of life; he must be like the man in Browning's fine poem " How it strikes a Contemporary," who walked about, took note of everything, looked at the new house building, poked his stick into the mortar.

> He stood and watched the cobbler at his trade,
> The man who slices lemons into drink,
> The coffee-roaster's brazier, and the boys
> That volunteer to help him turn its winch;
> He glanced o'er books on stalls with half an eye,
> And fly-leaf ballads on the vendor's string,
> And broad-edge bold-print posters by the wall;
> He took such cognisance of men and things!
> If any beat a horse, you felt he saw—
> If any cursed a woman, he took note,
> Yet stared at nobody—they stared at him,
> And found less to their pleasure than surprise,
> He seemed to know them, and expect as much.

ARTHUR CHRISTOPHER BENSON

That is the essayist's material; he may choose the scene, he may select the sort of life he is interested in, whether it is the street or the countryside or the sea-beach or the picture-gallery; but once there, wherever he may be, he must devote himself to seeing and realising and getting it all by heart. The writer must not be too much interested in the action and conduct of life. If he is a politician, or a soldier, or an emperor, or a plough-boy, or a thief, and is absorbed in what he is doing, with a vital anxiety to make profit or position or influence out of it; if he hates his opponents and rewards his friends; if he condemns, despises, disapproves, he at once forfeits sympathy and largeness of view. He must believe with all his might in the interest of what he enjoys, to the extent at all events of believing it worth recording and representing, but he must not believe too solemnly or urgently in the importance and necessity of any one sort of business or occupation. The eminent banker, the social reformer, the forensic pleader, the fanatic, the crank, the puritan—these are not the stuff out of which the essayist is made; he may have ethical preferences, but he must not indulge in moral indignation; he must be essentially tolerant, and he must discern quality rather than solidity. He must be concerned with the pageant of life, as it weaves itself with a moving tapestry of scenes and figures rather than with the aims and purposes of life. He must, in fact, be preoccupied with things as they appear, rather than with their significance or their ethical example.

THE ART OF THE ESSAYIST

I have little doubt in my own mind that the charm of the familiar essayist depends upon his power of giving the sense of a good-humoured, gracious and reasonable personality and establishing a sort of pleasant friendship with his reader. One does not go to an essayist with a desire for information, or with an expectation of finding a clear statement of a complicated subject; that is not the mood in which one takes up a volume of essays. What one rather expects to find is a companionable treatment of that vast mass of little problems and floating ideas which are aroused and evoked by our passage through the world, our daily employment, our leisure hours, our amusements and diversions, and above all by our relations with other people—all the unexpected, inconsistent, various simple stuff of life; the essayist ought to be able to impart a certain beauty and order into it, to delineate, let us say, the vague emotions aroused in solitude or in company by the sight of scenery, the aspect of towns, the impressions of art and books, the interplay of human qualities and characteristics, the half-formed hopes and desires and fears and joys that form so large a part of our daily thoughts. The essayist ought to be able to indicate a case or a problem that is apt to occur in ordinary life and suggest the theory of it, to guess what it is that makes our moods resolute or fitful, why we act consistently or inconsistently, what it is that repels or attracts us in our dealings with other people, what our private fancies are.

ARTHUR CHRISTOPHER BENSON

The good essayist is the man who makes a reader say: "Well, I have often thought all those things, but I never discerned before any connection between them, nor got so far as to put them into words." And thus the essayist must have a great and far-reaching curiosity; he must be interested rather than displeased by the differences of human beings and by their varied theories. He must recognise the fact that most people's convictions are not the result of reason, but a mass of associations, traditions, things half-understood, phrases, examples, loyalties, whims. He must care more about the inconsistency of humanity than about its dignity; and he must study more what people actually do think about than what they ought to think about. He must not be ashamed of human weaknesses or shocked by them, and still less disgusted by them; but at the same time he must keep in mind the flashes of fine idealism, the passionate visions, the irresponsible humours, the salient peculiarities, that shoot like sunrays through the dull cloudiness of so many human minds, and make one realise that humanity is at once above itself and in itself, and that we are greater than we know; for the interest of the world to the ardent student of it is that we most of us seem to have got hold of something that is bigger than we quite know how to deal with; something remote and far off, which we have seen in a distant vision, which we cannot always remember or keep clear in our minds. The supreme fact of human nature is its duality, its tendency to pull different ways, the tug-of-war between Devil and Baker which lies inside our restless brains. And the confessed aim of the essayist is to make people interested in life and in themselves and in the part they can take in life; and he does that best if he convinces men and women that life is a fine sort of a game, in which they can take a hand; and that every existence, however confined or restricted, is full of outlets and pulsing channels, and that the interest and joy of it is not confined to the politician or the millionaire, but is pretty fairly distributed, so long as one has time to attend to it, and is not preoccupied in some concrete aim or vulgar ambition.

Because the great secret which the true essayist whispers in our ears is that the worth of experience is not measured by what is called success, but rather resides in a fulness of life: that success tends rather to obscure and to diminish experience, and that we may miss the point of life by being too important, and that the end of it all is the degree in which we give rather than receive.

The poet perhaps is the man who sees the greatness of life best, because he lives most in its beauty and fineness. But my point is that the essayist is really a lesser kind of poet, working in simpler and humbler materials, more in the glow of life perhaps than in the glory of it, and not finding anything common or unclean.

The essayist is the opposite of the romancer, because his one and continuous aim is to keep the homely materials in view; to face actual conditions, not to fly from them. We think meanly of life if we believe that it has no sublime moments; but we think sentimentally of it if we believe that it has nothing but sublime moments. The essayist wants to hold the balance; and if he is apt to neglect the sublimities of life, it is because he is apt to think that they can take care of themselves; and that if there is the joy of adventure, the thrill of the start in the fresh air of the morning, the rapture of ardent companionship, the gladness of the arrival, yet there must be long spaces in between, when the pilgrim jogs steadily along, and seems to come no nearer to the spire on the horizon or to the shining embanked cloudland of the West. He has nothing then but his own thoughts to help him, unless he is alert to see what is happening in hedgerow and copse, and the work of the essayist is to make something rich and strange of those seemingly monotonous spaces, those lengths of level road.

Is, then, the Essay in literature a thing which simply stands outside classification, like Argon among the elements, of which the only thing which can be predicated is that it is there? Or like Justice in Plato's Republic, a thing which the talkers set out to define, and which ends by being the one thing left in a state when the definable qualities are taken away? No, it is not that. It is rather like what is called an organ prelude, a little piece with a theme, not very strict perhaps in form, but which can be fancifully treated, modulated from, and coloured

THE ART OF THE ESSAYIST

at will. It is a little criticism of life at some one point clearly enough defined.

We may follow any mood, we may look at life in fifty different ways—the only thing we must not do is to despise or deride, out of ignorance or prejudice, the influences which affect others; because the essence of all experience is that we should perceive something which we do not begin by knowing, and learn that life has a fulness and a richness in all sorts of diverse ways which we do not at first even dream of suspecting.

The essayist, then, is in his particular fashion an interpreter of life, a critic of life. He does not see life as the historian, or as the philosopher, or as the poet, or as the novelist, and yet he has a touch of all these. He is not concerned with discovering a theory of it all, or fitting the various parts of it into each other. He works rather on what is called the analytic method, observing, recording, interpreting, just as things strike him, and letting his fancy play over their beauty and significance; the end of it all being this: that he is deeply concerned with the charm and quality of things, and desires to put it all in the clearest and gentlest light, so that at least he may make others love life a little better, and prepare them for its infinite variety and alike for its joyful and mournful surprises.

A NOTE ON HENRY JAMES
By James Huneker

In company with other distinguished men who have passed away during the progress of the war, the loss of Henry James was passably chronicled. News from the various battle-fields took precedence over the death of a mere man of literary genius. This was to be expected. Nor need the fact be disguised that his secession from American citizenship may have increased the coolness which prevailed, still prevails, when the name of Mr. James is mentioned in print. More English than the English, he only practised what he preached, though tardily in the matter of his British naturalisation. That he did not find all the perfections in his native land is a personal matter; but that he should be neglected in favour of mediocrity is simply the penalty a great artist pays for his devotion to art. There is no need of indignation in the matter. Time rights such critical wrongs. Consider the case of Stendhal. The fiction of Henry James is for the future.

James seceded years ago from the English traditions, from Fielding, Dickens, Thackeray, and George Eliot. *The Wings of a Dove, The Ambassadors, The Golden Bowl* are fictions that will

A NOTE ON HENRY JAMES

influence future novelists. In our own days we see what a power James has been, a subtle breath on the waters of creation; Paul Bourget, Edith Wharton, even Joseph Conrad, and many minor English novelists. His later work, say, beginning with *The Tragic Muse,* is the prose equivalent of the seven arts in a revolutionary ferment. A marked tendency in the new movements is to throw overboard superfluous technical baggage. The James novel is one of grand simplifications.

As the symphony was modified by Liszt into the symphonic poem and later emerged in the shape of the tone-poem by Richard Strauss, so the novel of manners evolved from Flaubert's *Sentimental Education,* which, despite its "heavenly length," contains in solution all that the newer men have accomplished. Zola patterned after it in the prodigious Rougon-Macquart series; Daudet found therein the impressionism of his *Sapho* anticipated; Maupassant and Huysmans delved patiently and practised characteristic variations. Flaubert is the father of realism as he is part parent of symbolism. His excessive preoccupation with style and his attaching esoteric significance to words sound the note of symbolism. Now Henry James disliked *Sentimental Education*—like other great critics he had his blind side—yet he did not fail to benefit by the radical formal changes introduced by Flaubert, changes as revolutionary as those of Wagner in the music-drama. I call the later James novel a simplification. All the conventional chapter endings are dispensed with; many are suspended cadences. The accustomed and thrice-barren modulations from event to event are swept away; unprepared dissonances are of continual occurrence. There is no descriptive padding—that bane of second-class writers; nor are we informed at every speech of the name of a character. This elliptical method James absorbed from Flaubert, while his sometime oblique psychology is partly derived from Stendhal; indeed, without Stendhal both Meredith and James would have been sadly shorn of their psychological splendour. Nor is the shadow of Turgenev missing, not to mention that of Jane Austen.

Possibly the famous " third manner " of James was the result of his resorting to dictation; the pen inhibits where speech does not. These things make difficult reading for a public accustomed to the hypnotic passes of successful fiction-mongers. In James nothing is forestalled, nothing is obvious, one is for ever turning the curve of the unexpected. The actual story may be discouraging in its bareness, yet the situations are seldom fantastic. (The *Turn of the Screw* is an exception.) You rub your eyes as you finish; for with all your credulity, painful in its intensity, you have assisted at a pictorial evocation; both picture and evocation reveal magic in their misty attenuations. And there is ever the triumph of poetic feeling over banal sentiment. The portraiture in *Milly Theale* and *Maggie Verver* is clairvoyant. Milly's life is a miracle, her ending, art superlative. *The Wings of a Dove* is

A NOTE ON HENRY JAMES

filled with the faintly audible tread of destiny behind the arras of life. The reverberations are almost microphonic with here and there a crescendo or a climax. The spiritual string music of Henry James is more thrilling to the educated ear than the sound of the big drum and the blaring of trumpets. The implacable curiosity of the novelist concerning causes that do not seem final has been amply dealt with by Mr. Brownell. The question whether his story is worth the telling is a critical impertinence too often uttered; what most concerns us now in the James case is his manner, not his matter. All the rest is life.

As far as his middle period his manner is limpidity itself; the later style is a jungle of inversions, suspensions, elisions, repetitions, echoes, transpositions, transformations, neologisms, in which the heads of young adjectives despairingly gaze from afar at the verbs which come thundering at the close of sentences leagues long. It is bewildering, but more bewildering is this peculiarly individual style when draughted into smooth journalistic prose. Nothing remains. Henry James has not spoken. His dissonances cannot be resolved except in the terms of his own matchless art. His meanings evaporate when phrased in our vernacular. This may prove a lot of negating things, or it may not. Why prose should lag behind its sister arts I can't say; possibly because every pothouse politician is supposed to speak it. For that matter any one who has dipped into the well of English undefiled, seventeenth-century literature, must realise that nowadays we write a parlous prose. However, it is not a stately prose that James essayed. The son of a metaphysician and moralist—the writings of Henry James, the elder, are far from negligible—the brother of the greatest American psychologist, the late William James of brilliant memory, it need hardly be added that character problems are of more interest to this novelist than the external qualities of rhetorical sonority, or the fascination of glowing surfaces. You can no more read aloud a page of James than you can read aloud De Goncourt. For Flaubert, who modelled his magnificent prose harmonies on the Old Testament, Shakespeare, Bossuet, and Chateaubriand, the final test of noble prose is the audible reader thereof. Flaubert called it "spouting." The James prose appeals rather to the inner ear. Nuance and overtones not dazzling tropical hues or rhythmical variety. Henry James is a law unto himself. His novels may be a precursor of the books our grandchildren will enjoy when the hurly-burly of noisy adventure, cheap historical vapidities, and still cheaper drawing-room struttings shall have vanished. (But, like the poor, the stupid reader we shall always have with us.) In the fiction of the future a more complete synthesis will be attained. An illuminating essay by Arthur Symons places George Meredith among the decadents, the murderers of their mother tongue, the men who shatter syntax to serve their artistic ends. Henry James belonged to this group for a longer time than

A NOTE ON HENRY JAMES

the majority of his critics suspected. In his ruthless disregard of the niceties and conventionalities of sentence-structure I see the outcome of his dictation. Yet no matter how crabbed and involved is his page, a character always emerges from the smoke of his muttered enchantments. The chief fault is not his obscurity (his prose, like the prose in Browning's *Sordello*, is packed with too many meanings), but that his character always speaks in purest Jacobean. So do the people in Balzac's crowded, electric world. So the men and women of Dickens and Meredith. It is the fault—or virtue—of all subjective genius; however, not a fault or virtue of Flaubert or Turgenev or Tolstoy. All in all, Henry James is a distinctly American novelist, a psychologist of extraordinary power and divination. He has pinned to paper the soul of the cosmopolitan. The obsession of the moral problem that we feel in Hawthorne is not missing. Be his manner never so cryptic, his deep-veined humanity may be felt by those who read him aright. His Americans abroad suffer a deep-sea change; a complete gamut of achieved sensibility divides Daisy Miller from Maggie Verver. Henry James is a faithful Secretary to Society—the phrase is Balzac's—to the American afloat from his native mooring as well as at home. And his exquisite notations are the glory of English fiction.

Before me lies an autograph letter from Henry James to his friend Doctor Rice. It is dated 26th

JAMES HUNEKER

December, 1904, and the address 21 East Eleventh Street. It thus concludes: " I am not one of 'The Bostonians,' but was born in this city 15th April, 1843. Believe me, truly yours, Henry James." Although he died a naturalised Englishman, there seems to be some confusion as to his birthplace in the minds of his English critics. In Ford Madox Hueffer's critical study, *Henry James*, we read on page 95 that the life of James "began in New England in 1843." He was born in America in 1843, then a land where culture was rare. That delightful condescension in foreigners is still extant. Now this isn't such a serious matter, for Henry James was a citizen of the world; but the imputation of a New England birthplace does matter, because it allows the English critic—and how many others?—to perform variations on the theme of Puritanism, the Puritanism of his art. James as a temperamental Puritan—one is forced to capitalise the unhappy word! Apart from the fact that there is less Puritanism in New England than in the Middle West, James is not a Puritan. He does not possess the famous New England conscience. He would have been the first to repudiate the notion. For him the Puritan temperament has a "faintly acrid perfume." To ascribe to Puritanism the seven deadly virtues and refinement, sensibility, intellectuality, is a common enough mistake. James never made that mistake. He knew that all the good things of life are not in the exclusive possession of the Puritans. He must not be identified with the

A NOTE ON HENRY JAMES

case he studies. Strictly speaking, while he was on the side of the angels, like all great artists, he is not a moralist; indeed, he is our first great "immoralist," a term that has supplanted the old-fashioned amoralist. And he wrote the most unmoral short story in the English language, one that also sets the spine trilling because of its supernatural element as never did Poe, or De Maupassant.

Another venerable witticism, which has achieved the pathos of distance, was made a quarter of a century ago by George Moore. Mr. Moore said: "Henry James went to France and read Turgenev. W. D. Howells stayed at home and read Henry James." To lend poignancy to this mild epigram Mr. Hueffer misquotes it, substituting the name of De Maupassant for Turgenev's. A rather uncanny combination—Henry and Guy. A still more aged "wheeze" bobs up in the pages of Mr. Hueffer. Need we say that it recites the ancient saw about William James, the fictionist, and his brother Henry, the psychologist. None of these things is in the least true. With the prudishness and peanut piety of puritanism Henry James has nothing in common. He did not alone read Turgenev, he met him and wrote of him with more sympathy and understanding than he did of Flaubert or Baudelaire; and Mr. Howells never wrote a page that resembled either the Russian's or the American's fiction. Furthermore, James is a masterly psychologist and a tale-teller. To the credit of his latest English critics this is acknowledged, and generously.

JAMES HUNEKER

Mr. Hueffer is an accomplished craftsman in many literary fields, he writes with authority, though too often in a superlative key. But how James would have winced when he read in Mr. Hueffer's book that he is or was "the greatest of living men." This surely is a planet-struck phrase. The Hueffer study is stuffed with startling things. He bangs Balzac over the head. He tells the truth about Flaubert, whose *Sentimental Education* is an entire Human Comedy. He thinks ill of "big business," that "business and whatever takes place 'down-town' or in the city is simply not worth the attention of any intelligent being. It is a matter of dirty little affairs incompetently handled by men of the lowest class of intelligence." But all this in a volume about the most serene and luminous intelligence of our times. Mr. Hueffer also "goes for" James as critic. He once dared to couple the name of the "odious" George Eliot with Flaubert's. It does rather take the breath away, but, after all, didn't the tolerant and catholic critic who was Henry James say that no one is constrained to like any particular kind of writing? As to the "cats and monkeys, monkeys and cats—all human life is there," of *The Madonna of the Future*, we need not take the words as a final message; nor are the other phrases quoted: "The soul is immortal certainly —if you've got one, but most people haven't! Pleasure would be right if it were pleasure right through, but it never is." Mr. Hueffer says that James "found English people who were just people singularly nasty," and who can say him nay after reading *The Sacred Fount*? But he ends on the right note: " And for a man to have attained to international rank with phrases intimately national is the supreme achievement of writers—a glory that is reserved only for the Dantes, the Goethes, and the Shakespeares, who none the less remain supremely national." Neither Mr. Hueffer nor Miss West is in doubt as to the essential Americanism of Henry James. He is almost as American as Howells, who is our Anthony Trollope, plus style and vision. And Trollope, by the way, will loom larger in the future despite his impersonality and microscopic manner.

The James art is Cerebral Comedy, par excellence. To alter his own words, he plays his intellectual instrument to perfection. He is a portraitist doubled by a psychologist. His soul is not a solitary pool in a midnight forest, but an unruffled lake, sun-smitten or cloud-shadowed; yet in whose depths there is a moving mass of exquisite living things. His pages reverberate with the under hum of humanity. We may not exactly say of him as Hazlitt said of Walter Scott: " His works, taken altogether, are almost like a new edition of human nature." But we can follow with the coda of that same dictum: " This is indeed to be an author." Many more than the dozen superior persons mentioned by Huysmans enjoy the James novels. His swans are not always immaculate, but they are not " swans of the cesspool," to quote Landor. There is never an odour of leaking gas in his premises, as he once remarked of the D'Annunzio fiction. He has the cosmopolitan soul. There is no slouch in his spiritual gait. Like Renan, he abhorred the "horrible mania of certitude" to be found in the writing of his realistic contemporaries. He does not always dot the "i's" of his irony, a subrisive irony. But the spiritual antennæ which he puts forth so tentatively always touch real things, not conjectural. And what tactile sense he boasts. He peeps into the glowing core of emotion, but seldom describes it. His ears are for overtones, not the brassy harmonies of the obvious, of truths, flat and flexible. Yet what novelist has kept his ear so close to quotidian happenings, and with what dignity and charm in his crumbling cadences? Not even that virtuoso of the ugly, Huysmans, than whom no writer of the past century ever "rendered" surfaces into such impeccable truth, with such implacable ferocity, is as clairvoyant as James.

Fustian and thunder form no part of the James stories, which are like a vast whispering gallery, the dim reverberations of which fill the listening ear. He is an "auditive" as well as a "visualist," to employ the precious classification of the psychiatrists. His astute senses tell him of a world which we are only beginning to comprehend. He is never obscure, never recondite; but, like Browning, he sends a veritable multiplex of ideas along a single wire. Mr. Howells has rightly said of him that it is not well to pursue the meanings of an

A NOTE ON HENRY JAMES

author to the very heart of darkness. However, readers as a rule like their fiction served on a shiny plate; above all, they don't like a story to begin in one key and end in another. If it's to be pork and molasses or " hog and hominy " (George Meredith's words), then let it be these delectable dishes through every course. But James is ever in modulation. He tosses his theme ballwise in the air, and while its spirals spin and bathe in the blue he weaves a web of gold and lace, and it is marvellously spun. He is more atmospheric than linear. His theme is shown from a variety of angles, but the result is synthetic. Elizabeth Luther Cary has pointed out that he is not a remorseless analyst. He does not take the mechanism of his marionette apart, but lets us examine it in completeness. As a psychologist he stands midway between Stendhal and Turgenev. He interprets feeling, rather than fact.

Like our sister planet, the moon, he has his rhythmic moments of libration; he then reveals his other side, a profoundly human, emotional one. He is not all frosty intellect. But he holds in horror the facile expression of the sentiments. It's only too easy to write for those avid of sentimentalism, or to express what Thomas Huxley calls " sensualistic caterwauling." In the large, generous curve of his temperament there is room for all life, but not for a lean or lush statement of life. You may read him in a state of mellow exasperation, but you cannot deny his ultimate sincerity. There is no lack of substance in his densely woven patterns, for patterns there are, though the figure be difficult to piece out. His route of emerald is elliptical; follow him who dare! A "wingy mystery." He is all vision. He does not always avoid naked issues. His thousand and one characters are significantly vital. His is not "the shadow land of American fiction"; simply his supreme tact of omission has dispensed with the entire banal apparatus of fiction as commonly practised. To use a musical example: his prose is like the complicated score of some latter-day composer, and his art, like music, is a solvent. He discards lumbering descriptions, antique melodramatics, set developments and dénouements, mastodonic structures. The sharp savour of character is omnipresent. His very pauses are eloquent. He evokes. His harmonic tissue melts into remoter harmonic perspectives. He composes in every tonality. Continuity of impression is unfailing. When reading him sympathetically one recalls the saying of Maurice Barrès: "For an accomplished spirit there is but one dialogue, that between our two egos—the momentary ego that we are and the ideal one toward which we strive." For Jacobeans this interior dialogue, with its "secondary intention," marches like muted music through the pages of the latter period. Henry James will always be a touchstone for the tasteless.

A DEAD MAN
By J C. Squire

The screaming of the gale had dwindled into a fitful grumbling; the recurrent boom and crash and hiss of the sleepless North Sea on the shingle below the cottage was soothing by contrast with the wild elemental tumult that had been filling the hours after twilight. The little window had ceased to rattle; the fire had pulled itself together and the lamp burnt up comfortably. Probably the inhabitants of the fishermen's hovels around had all gone to bed long ago; the knowledge of that, I cannot tell why, added to my feeling of seclusion. In an armchair, with my dressing-gown around me, a pipe in my left hand and a glass of warm liquor within reach of my right, I settled down to the familiar book. It had been my periodic, though never my continual companion during my later schooldays and ever since. Given quiet and solitude, it had always the power of taking me, without effort or delay, into another world.

Did I still smoke and feel the warm fire about my knees? In a mechanical way; but my essential self was elsewhere. Here was a world where shadows walked more vivid and grim than any

J. C. SQUIRE

mundane creature, a sunless land reeking with heavy vapours and populated with monstrous shapes of disease and misery and sin. Here there were dark caves where the soul was a prey to infamous insects; grey fields hissing at the beat of straight pillars of unending rain; black lakes writhing with hideous coils, abysmal woods, and winds that howled desolately around the graves of the unhappy dead. Here, in a slimy soil, full of pits and broken implements, lay great disjected limbs, fragments of terrible marble splendour, half buried in dark festering ground whence sprang only rare clusters of heavy and venomous blooms. Old blind men and women groped by mouldering damp walls; miserable taverns, ill-furnished and lit with smoky lanterns, accommodated companies of the damned, ferocious and wretched, gambling at faded green tables or holding haggard revels with outworn courtesans. Everywhere, beneath a sky as merciless as iron, walked the poet, his shoulders bowed, his strong head thrust forward in an intense and melancholy curiosity. His profound eyes under their weary and compassionate lids burned with a sombre lustre; his wide firm mouth with its projecting lower lip wore an expression of imperial sadness, of amusement without joy, tenderness without illusion, and pity without hope.

Rocks, darkness, blood, poisonous fungi, the oily scales of gigantic snakes, rotting bodies dead and alive, lovely things gone purulent and a prey to armies of worms: these things he beheld around

A DEAD MAN

him, and Remorse, Gloom and Despair flew their sable standards on the battlements of his brain. Yet as he lived in this nightmare country the measure of its horror and infamy was the measure of the sweetness of terrestrial regions and forms he had seen and would not see again and of spiritual fountains he had always thirsted for and would never know. With courteous and precise cynicism on his lips, he thought of quiet virginal chambers, of waters singing under the moon, of terraces where taintless music sobbed into the open night, of pure maternal mistresses with protecting arms and vigilant eyes, of fields slumbering in the sunlight, of leagues of ocean heaving under warm tremulous heavens, of hot ports, gorgeous and perfumed, where forests of masts sprang by the blazing quays, and palm-trees grew to the verge of the glittering blue waters. And in more purged and abstract mood he would dream of divine Beauty, throned in plains of inaccessible azure, remote from the squalor and vice of the actual, sublimely placid, Beauty who never smiled and never wept. . . .

The lamp burned more dimly, and I closed the book. Chin on hands, elbows on knees, I stared into the sleepy fire and thought of him. He had died long before I was born, after complete paralysis had immured him, a living corpse, for many months. Nevertheless I knew each line of his face, each expression of his features, every subtle inflexion of his inner voice, every pang that gnawed at his breast. I could not conceive that dissolution could touch him or that death could work a change in him. I felt that his spirit was eternal and constant, more durable and more certain than the stars and their systems. So I mused, as I had done from time to time for years.

With a start and a swift fearful throbbing of the blood I sat up and sharply turned. Was it a step behind me?

The flames softly lapped and the coals made pin-point crackles; outside in the darkness the sea still boomed and washed on the shingle. Everything in the corner by the stair was in its place; the fire shone as usual on the edges of chair and box and picture frame. Yet my heart shook and my limbs stiffened and the scalp under my hair tingled chill as if at the touch of supernatural fingers; for I knew there was something in the corner, an inaudible sound, an invisible cloud.

Dry-lipped I spoke. I did not hear but, as it were, felt an answer. It was he; I knew it and my fear fell off me like a cold sheet; gently joyous I whispered his name.

Sensible of nothing else, I looked at the place where I knew he stood. With effortless mental vision I saw him. Nothing of him had altered; the broad brow, the profound eyes, the firm and melancholy mouth. I had no need to speak again. He could read every thought, every friendly impulse that brought tears of glad sorrow into my eyes. Around his lips there hovered the wistfully cynical smile of one who mocked all things and himself most of all, and pitied all things but himself least. He had come for a friend through a door, unlocked, for all I know, never before or since. But though the smile still floated around his lips, his deep eyes, when he perceived my voiceless inquiry, were for a moment hard with unmingled suffering. It was as though in his formal polite way he was speaking: "I am who I was and where I was. I long for the things I have never seen and those I shall never see again. The beauty I find is evil and pestilent; the beauty I search for I shall not find. The springs of the milky way are salt to my palate as the rivers of the earth; and like the apples of life, the golden stars have turned to ashes in my hand."

The shadowy air in the room quivered. Solitude most evident poured over me. I knew he had gone away, the hunger for the unattainable in his heart, a lonely voyager faring for ever through an alien universe.

I felt as though my body did not belong to me. With an arm on the mantelpiece, I kicked moodily at the fender; then with an automatic laugh I prepared to go to bed. There was no desire of any kind left in me.

THE LONELY AUTHOR
By J. C. Squire

I HAD left my friends, had rather a long journey before me, and thought I would break it. Halfway there was a cathedral town, a few miles from which is a house where I counted on being put up for the night. But I had left it too late. A tardy telegram produced the reply that everybody was away, so I was left stranded. "Very well," I thought, "I will go to a hotel." This I did, but, the pleasures of the table exhausted, the hotel provided no others. There was no billiard room, and the guests were all of that sort of restless and self-centred birds of passage with whom it is impossible to enter into conversation, much less get up a four. When I had read the newspaper cuttings about royal visits to the hostelry and the times at which the stage coaches used to leave it for London in Lord North's day, I was left without occupation. Like a fool, I had forgotten to get anything to read, having not a single volume with me except the latest cheap volume of *Tarzan* from which I had drained the last drop of honey—or, should I say, blood—in the train. With my most insinuating smile, I attempted to borrow something from the lady in the office. She had nothing, but told me that the whole library of the hotel was in the Resident Visitors' Smoking Lounge. My spirits rose, and I went to that room. It was a very odd collection. There were about twenty volumes in all, including the corpses of old Bradshaws from which the vital spark of utility had long since departed. Even I, omnivorous reader as I count myself, cannot hoax myself into curiosity about the time at which the fast trains got to Bristol in 1888. But the other volumes were not much more alive to me. I shut as soon as I had opened the grimy bound volumes of the *Magazine of Art*; the *Temple Bar* did not detain me. The few novels were all books which I had read long since and did not wish to read again, *John Halifax, Gentleman*, being the most notable. There remained three things of some interest. The first was an old green book about English Freshwater Fish, the second an odd (and not the first) volume of an extremely long and tedious analysis of Edmund Spenser's poetry, and the third an inscribed copy—I supposed somebody had left it there—of a long political poem by William Allingham. Allingham's signature interested me, and I have liked some of his shorter poems, but one or two pages of this laborious narrative made it plain to me that even the brown trout, the chub, the dace and the roach had more charms for me than Allingham's blank verse. So with a discontented sigh I got my coat and hat and went out into the frosty moonlit night. After all, oughtn't a man of sensibility to be content with a cathedral town under the moon?

It certainly was beautiful. There was no traffic, and the few pedestrians slunk quietly through the shadows. In the narrow streets the lamps lit up old timbered fronts, gables, and overhung upper stories. The river, with a moon reflected in it, ran quietly under the old stone bridge, overhung by willows insubstantial in the moonshine. Here and there one had peeps of the towers of the cathedral, and at last I came upon the lawns around it whence its huge bulk, shadowed with buttresses and statuary, rose ghostly to the sky. But passing under an archway I came upon a wide enclosed place of shining grass surrounded with long Georgian houses, faintly porticoed and trellised. Through the lit yellow blinds of their upper windows came, as I walked, sounds of one music succeeding another, a piano, a violin, a voice. It was cold and the place deserted, and it was then that I fell to statistics.

For I was feeling cold and lonely. It was still, by my standards, early. I didn't want to go back to the faded carpets, the varnish, the stuffiness, the tawdry sitting-room and bleak bedroom of that very historic hotel. I wanted talk and company, and in all that town there was nobody to whom I had, I thought, a right to speak. But nobody? It suddenly occurred to me that I was an author, an author of books. Not a very popular author, not an author who counts his sales—much less his receipts—by tens of thousands; but an author nevertheless whose

THE LONELY AUTHOR

works have to some extent penetrated the educated population. For the first time in my life, as my footsteps rang again down an empty and thrice-traversed High Street, I made a computation as to the gross total of all my volumes which had been purchased by the public. There were so many thousands. The population of the United Kingdom was, say, fifty millions. Take the average number of my volumes owned by each of my patrons as two, assume the population of that town to be twenty-five thousand; the deduction was that—and as it was a cathedral city, full of learned people, the chances were nominally in my favour—in at least two or three houses of that town there existed copies of my books bought, paid for, probably read, possibly liked by the inhabitants. But which houses?

Here was I, solitary and chilled. Yet, perhaps, in the very house I was passing, whose curtains gave me a peep of mahogany, old silver and books, there must be one or two strangers within a few minutes of me who might even be glad were I to walk suddenly in upon them. I had never heard their names; yet to them, for such is the magic of authorship, to them if to nobody else in the whole town, even my Christian names were familiar, possibly my age, the outlines of my education, the development of the talents they were generous enough to have perceived in me. I attempted to picture what they might be like. I had glimpses of a cultivated doctor who collected books, of a plump canon's intelligent son home for the vacation, of a pair of

J. C. SQUIRE

spinster ladies, with wise eyes and greying hair, living at peace amid charming furniture, reading a well-chosen parcel from Mudie's every week. Whatever they were like, there they must have been. Possibly you, reader, were yourself one of them, and would have been delighted at one—I can't promise you would have liked more than one —visit from so congenial an artist. But I passed your door with a sound of footsteps like any other; I heard the murmur of your voice like the murmur of any other voice; I saw the portico of your house for the first time and the last, and have now forgotten it. Had you accidentally come to the door I might have spoken. As it was I went back to the hotel and was bored.

WALTER BAGEHOT
By George Sampson

The writer of literary miscellanies is a suspected person. For casual skimming in a weekly or monthly review he is all very well; but has he any right to the comparative eternity of publishers' cloth? His matter smells of the common-place book, his method suggests the pump-handle. He thinks in paragraphs, sorts the world into pages, and sees men as columns walking. We doubt his authority; he writes, but does he know? The first essential of good writing is the having of something to say, a condition often unfulfilled in the case of the miscellaneous author. Knowledge is the mother of eloquence in literature, just as, unfortunately, necessity is the mother of invention. If you are to transfer something of life into your book, you must know life and not merely the vital statistics accessible in the books of others. An original writer is inspired by life, an imitative author by literature. The one reports at first hand, the other at second, or fifth, hand. The work of the one is vital, the work of the other vitiated by inbreeding and the consumption of breathed air.

GEORGE SAMPSON

Thus the better part of the world prefers its men of letters to be men of experience as well, and not mere literary dilettanti who shrink from contact with reality. How far the preference is sound can be decided by a rapid review of the varied, and sometimes tumultuous careers of many great writers.

Now this is specially applicable to the case of Walter Bagehot, first because he was a miscellaneous writer who has survived by his fitness, next because he happened to be a distinguished man of affairs as well as a distinguished man of letters, and next because he has expressed, in his own incisive way, the general sense of the world in such matters. Shakespeare is to him a type of the "experiencing mind" with a store of first-hand observation as material, while Southey represents the mere man of letters, the literary manufacturer, who lived in a vacuum, and with painful industry wrote poetry before breakfast, philosophy before lunch, and history before dinner. Certainly there was no keener man of the world than Bagehot himself. He knew men, he knew politics, he knew business; and that knowledge is revealed in all he wrote. His essays are alive because he was alive; his financial theory is intelligent because he was a financier in practice; and his constitutional philosophy is sound because he knew both politics and politicians. Without "the vision and the faculty divine," mere experience is of course almost valueless in literature; but with "the accomplishment of words," experience makes a powerful combination.

WALTER BAGEHOT

Bagehot (whose name, by the way, should be pronounced as if written Badge-ot) was born at Langport in Somerset on 3rd February, 1826, of distinguished banking lineage. His father was managing director and vice-chairman of the famous Stuckey's Bank, whose notes were so familiar in the West of England that true Somerset men have been know to reject the foreign and suspicious paper of Threadneedle Street and to demand payment " in Stuckey." Indeed, there was finance on both sides of the family, for his mother was also a Stuckey; and she contributed to the joint stock not only further banking traditions, but a highly cultivated interest of her own and of her relatives in scientific inquiry and pursuits. The future author of *Physics and Politics* certainly owed much of his keen interest in scientific speculation to the influence of his maternal relatives. He was educated first at a Bristol school, and then at University College, London, where one of his friends was R. H. Hutton, afterwards editor of the *Spectator*, whose charming memorial essay is the chief authority for details of Bagehot's life. He took the mathematical scholarship with his Bachelor's degree at London University in 1846, and the gold medal in Intellectual and Moral Philosophy with his Master's degree two years later. These distinctions indicate some of the predilections and influences of his youth, but, as usual, much should be set down to the account of time and place. Bagehot's most impressionable years were spent in London and during the forties, with Cobden and Newman as the main lines of influence. The family Unitarianism that prevented him from going to Oxford must be counted as a fortunate circumstance; for to such a mind as Bagehot's the "now" of London was better than the "once" of Oxford. He did not, however, completely escape the influence of Oxford, for that lovely city with its remote and cloistral atmosphere was personified in John Henry Newman, whose winsome poetry captivated Bagehot, as so many more, and compelled him to an interest in the problems that troubled Rome's most distinguished convert.

To a temperament like Bagehot's, the merely sentimental appeal of Rome counted for something, but not for much. That it had an effect certain verses remain to prove; but this disturbance is an almost inevitable phase—sometimes the first, sometimes the last phase—of the religious mind; and Bagehot's possession of a religious mind is proved by the fact that his views underwent a change. That the change, from the orthodox point of view, was in the direction of breadth rather than intensity makes no difference. The unquestioning acceptance of a form of faith as a sort of geographical circumstance is a mark, not of the religious, but of the merely passive mind. The challenging and the changing of early religious prepossessions is at least a sign that the mind has been troubled by deep matters, and is anxious for the truth. While, then, the sentimental aspect of Rome had some effect upon Bagehot, the real secret of its attraction lay in the historical, the pragmatic glamour of the Catholic Church. Rome, to him, was a polity justified, on the whole, by its consequences. A constitutional system that had worked through a past of wonderful history and continued to work in a changed and changing present, would certainly seem to deserve the respect, and almost the adherence, of a mind predisposed to political considerations.

Fortunately, however, Newman was not the sole interest of his college years. London was ringing with the strife of Free Trade against Protection; and whatever else this question may have been, it was certainly actual and vital. Whether the Church of Rome was the rightful representative of the primitive apostolic foundation was no doubt an important matter; but whether bread should be too dear to buy had at least an appearance of superior urgency. It was a primitive question of a different kind. Bagehot and Hutton pursued Cobden and Bright and other Free Trade heroes in their oratorical progress, and diligently discussed their speeches by the standards of Chatham and Burke. The enthusiasm thus enkindled never died away. Free Trade remained with Bagehot as a real dynamic interest, the charm of Newman asserting itself rather as a sentimental, literary influence; so that, to take an instance of their divergence, Sir Robert Peel, who presently became little better than one of the ungodly to Newman and his kind, commanded Bagehot's increasing respect, and is the subject of appreciative consideration in one of his best essays.

In the friendship between Bagehot and that most tragic of Newman's disciples, Arthur Hugh Clough, something of the master's influence may perhaps be seen; but the common interest was philosophical rather than theological, and the connection was actually formed in the unecclesiastical atmosphere of University College, to which Clough had come as Principal of a hall of residence. Between Clough, with his cloistral instincts thwarted by sceptical convictions, and Bagehot, with his sanguine, practical interest in the world of men, there would seem, at first sight, to be no point of contact; but the philosophic quietism of Clough found an answer in the younger man's instinctive dislike of extremes, especially of emotional extremes; and their actual literary practice suggests a further likeness. They were both serious men with a vein of humour that tinged their wisdom, now with gaiety and now with cynicism. The sardonic asides of the Literary Studies find a counterpart in such poems as *The Latest Decalogue*; and if Bagehot is one of our most high-spirited essayists, *The Bothie of Tober-na-Vuolich* is one of our most pleasant pieces of poetic gaiety. The strength of the friendship is but feebly indicated in Bagehot's chilly essay on the poet, which has even more than the writer's usual restraint upon his feelings, and dissipates at the end, as if he were afraid of opening his heart, into a rather superfluous account of the *Amours de Voyage*. For the truth about Clough it is not to this essay by one of his closest friends that we must turn.

In 1851 Bagehot went to Paris and lived through the stirring times of the *coup d'état* by which the President, Louis Napoleon, overthrew the Republic, and secured the perpetuation of his power under the title of Napoleon III., Emperor of the French. Bagehot's cynical and unexpected approval of this political crime was expressed in a series of letters that appalled his friends and almost extinguished the respectable Unitarian paper to which he had been rashly asked to contribute. He was not quite twenty-six; he was of the eager, sanguine temperament whose defect it is to run into cocksureness; his Liberalism (such as it was) did not at any time of his life exclude a whole-hearted contempt for the masses: hence his rather Nietzschean approval of Louis Napoleon—really a man of sawdust, yet, at the moment, strong enough, as it seemed, to tread down the mutable many who, being French, were silly precisely because they were not stupid. "I think M. Bonaparte," he writes in a letter to Hutton, "is entitled to great praise. He has very good heels to his boots, and the French just want treading down, and nothing else—calm, cruel, businesslike oppression, to take the dogmatic conceit out of their heads." And so, with characteristic cynicism, and with characteristic eagerness for experience, Bagehot helped the Republicans, whom he despised, to build barricades against the man whom he admired

GEORGE SAMPSON

This episode of his early manhood is additional evidence of the hardness that somewhat mars his work—hardness, remember, not bluntness. His temper was of steel—keen, resilient, but undeniably hard. He seemed impatient of emotion and suspicious of any action born of its influence. He was, in fact, an example of excessive rationalism; and the defect of excessive rationalism is that it is excessively unreasonable. Reason looks well on paper; but in reality we have scanty grounds for assuming that reason is a better guide to life than feeling. Reason is certainly triumphant, and feeling as certainly annihilated in the science with which, in his lifetime, Bagehot's name was specially connected. He was a financier and economist. While he admired Adam Smith (upon whom he has written a very delightful essay), his respect for Ricardo was warmer still. Now the defect (or merit—so much depends upon point of view) of Ricardo and his school is that they dehumanised what is after all a matter of human concern. They wrote as if the world were peopled by man and not by men, and as if that world were the fictitious realm of pure mechanics, where elasticity is perfect, where friction is unknown, and where you may always neglect the weight of the elephant. Bagehot recognised quite fully this serious limitation of economic science, and defended it as a necessary method of inquiry. From that point of view he is right; but in this study, almost beyond any other, there is a constant temptation to take abstractions as realities. No one could live in the rigid, frictionless world of pure mechanics; yet people constantly talk, and even act, as if we did live in the world of pure economics. After all, the father of the science was wiser than his followers when he called his treatise *The Wealth of Nations*, and considered his subject, not as a separate entity, but as a mere aspect of the whole human science into the scheme of which he tried to fit it. Bagehot suffered from economic degeneration of the heart. For the " still, sad music of humanity " he had no ear. Shakespeare's scorn of the rude mechanicals is music to him, and in any discussion of capital and labour, he is not only on the side of capital—as he might reasonably be, but he is patently contemptuous of labour, as no true economist should be. Here again the abstractions of science are a source of confusion. Much of the absurdity that results from argument about capital and labour is due to our incorrigible dialectic habit of dividing things into two abstract and mutually exclusive parts, and then assuming that the abstractions are facts. Labour does no more in the world's work, Bagehot argues in the *Economic Studies*, than the compositors do in producing *The Times*; whereas Capital is like the editor who, by shaping a policy, choosing this, and rejecting that, actually makes the paper. This would be a hard world for most of us, if we had to be judged by our metaphors; but that Bagehot was satisfied with such an illustration shows the depth of unreality into which a pure economist can sink; for he overlooks not only the fact that the editor, as such, is already part of the labour, but this: that if the editor could (as in fact he cannot) dispense with all assistance, and produce and distribute the paper single-handed, he would cease to be part of the labour, and become all of it. The economist, even more than the author, is a person who lives in a vacuum and takes no account of mankind.

Bagehot had at first intended to practise at the Bar, to which he was called in 1852; but during his stay in Paris he abandoned the career of "law and bad jokes till we are forty" (as Dizzy has it), and began serious work at the family calling. Business, he said, is more amusing than pleasure; and he gravely declared that dabbling his hands in a heap of sovereigns was a certain cure for the megrims. His amusing business fortunately did not engross all his energies, for he found time to write a series of articles for the *Prospective Review* and the *National*—the latter of which he assisted in editing. His marriage in 1858 to a daughter of the Right Hon. James Wilson, founder of the *Economist*, was a factor of much importance in his life; for, apart from the domestic happiness that ensued, the connection with Wilson gave him an inside intimacy with the world of high politics. When his father-in-law went to India as Financial Member of the Council, Bagehot succeeded him in the editorial chair of the *Economist*, and held it till his own death in 1877. Politics had always been a strong

WALTER BAGEHOT

interest of the Bagehot family; moreover politics and finance are near neighbours—when they are not the same thing. As editor of the *Economist* Bagehot came into closer touch with the machine and gained the knowledge of its working that helps to give his little book on the Constitution a classic authority.

There is little more to say of Bagehot's external life. He tried more than once to get into Parliament, but was never actually returned. On the whole this is well. He belonged really to neither of the great parties. He was, to use his own phrase, "between sizes in politics." He was a vigorous Free Trader and could never have worked with a Tory party that still hankered after Protection, and he was too remote from sympathy with democracy ever to have been a good Liberal. For us this detachment is pure gain, and makes him, in his political essays, the friendly foe of Conservatives and the "damned good-natured friend" of Liberals. His robust mind was housed in an apparently robust body—though far less robust than was imagined, for he died suddenly on 24th March, 1877, at the early age of fifty-one.

Bagehot's work has the brilliance of a diamond; but it has also its adamantine hardness. This is generally a defect of the critical spirit. Where criticism ends and creation begins would evade the nicest of definitions. In a sense, all literature is criticism, since it is an account of how life strikes an observer. Learned gentlemen of the academic type, accustomed to the pigeon-holing of literature, have been driven to querulous discontent by Matthew Arnold's dictum that poetry is a criticism of life. But Arnold's judgment was sound, and was wrong only in being restricted. Not poetry alone, but all literature, all great literature, is a criticism of life. However, though we may not be able to state the difference in a definition, yet we feel that that there is a kind of literature that is critical rather than creative. To the category of criticism all Bagehot's work belongs. He is the purely critical spirit of the mid-Victorian era as Samuel Butler was of its close. To borrow a phrase from his own world, he audited the accounts of politics and letters, and wrote a vigorous report on the balance or deficit. Now the perfect accountant is passionless, and therefore sometimes grotesquely wrong. Not long ago, a government auditor, in reviewing the accounts of an education authority responsible for the feeding of necessitous children, reported adversely upon the expenditure of money in apples and bananas. A child, it appeared, might have an apple in a dumpling, for that was food and therefore a necessity; but not an apple by itself, for that was fruit and therefore a luxury. It is in just such a way as this that the critical spirit goes wrong. As a general fact, no writer creates according to rule—those who, like Wordsworth, think they do, being unaware of the difference between their impulses and their intentions; but many writers criticise according to rules, and have thereby brought criticism at times into a contempt that might have killed it, if the passion for sitting in judgment had not been as eternal in the human breast as hope. The man or book that fulfils the requirements of *a priori* criticism is generally salt that has not lost, but has never had, a savour. Thus Bagehot thought nothing of Abraham Lincoln and a great deal of Sir George Lewis. Here I am afraid it is necessary to warn a present-day reader against thinking immediately of Ely Place and society scandal. The Sir George Lewis of Bagehot's admiration was not the eminent solicitor, but Sir George Cornewall Lewis, author of treatises on ancient astronomy, ancient history and ancient languages; Secretary to the Treasury, Chancellor of the Exchequer, and War Secretary in successive Palmerston ministries, and altogether as completely dead as it is possible for a departed statesman to be. Such are the idols that rationalist criticism sets up for worship. Bagehot was at fault, too, with greater men. While he says true things of Disraeli, he talks of that statesman's lack of influence over Englishmen in terms that every Primrose Day disproves; and his forecast of Gladstone's future certainly contains no hint of the now almost legendary "Grand Old Man." Bagehot's auditing of literary and political accounts is undeniably vigorous, and with complete impartiality he was ready to vivisect his friends as if he loved them. Yet it is well to remind ourselves that the man who is moved by his feelings is not commonly more at fault than the man who is moved by his logic, and he has the advantage of being wrong more amiably.

But all this is the defect and not the essence of Bagehot's quality. In actual fact he is the most inspiriting of writers, as full of humour as of wisdom. No truer thing could be said of him than the remark, quoted by Hutton, that he made one either think or laugh,—usually both. He has all Macaulay's clearness, and if he has less than Macaulay's force, he has more than Macaulay's humour, and more than Macaulay's depth. He is a geniunely original writer, with a power of showing his subject from new standpoints. You have seen pictures of cathedral interiors with central aisle bisecting the nave into precisely similar halves and leading straight to a tiny altar in the middle of the composition. Bagehot gives you no such view. His, rather, is the art that reveals a subject in illuminative glimpses from unexpected corners— here a strange vista, there a remote tomb, here the quaintly chiselled saint, there the incongruous gargoyle. The image is heavy, but it will serve; for in all he wrote there is an element of the unexpected. His bright phrases flash not only on the surface but into the depths of his subject. As an essayist (and he is essentially that) Bagehot's popularity is perceptibly increasing. He has, in a degree quite remarkable in an Englishman, the quality that the French call *esprit*; and, like the French, he was not afraid to use in writing the cultivated spoken language of his countrymen. Indeed, many passages of the essays have all the easy intimacy and sparkle of first-rate conversation, as far removed from the pompous and the forced as from the slangy and the slip-shod. But he is not merely amusing. His note of mingled gravity and levity is quite his own. He can be as cynical and worldly as you please, as in his vivid letters on the *coup d'état*, and just as other-worldly in the essays and asides that touch upon the perilous topics of faith and morals. He is thus a grateful writer to the ordinary man. We are neither beasts nor angels. Our feet are planted on the earth, but our eyes scan the heavens; and so we are glad of a writer who knows our limitations and our aspirations and is kind to both.

RICHARD JEFFERIES' "AMARYLLIS AT THE FAIR"

By Edward Garnett

"The book is not a novel" is a phrase often in the mouth of critics, who on second thoughts might, perhaps, add with less emphasis, "it does not conform to the common type of novel." Fortified, however, with that sense of rectitude that dictates conformity to our neighbours and a safe acquiescence in the mysterious movements of public taste, Victorian critics have exclaimed with touching unanimity—" What a pity Jefferies tried to write novels! Why didn't he stick to essays in natural history!"

What a pity Jefferies should have given us *Amaryllis at the Fair*, and *After London*! This opinion has been propagated with such fervency that it seems almost a pity to disturb it by inquiring into the nature of these his achievements. Certainly the critics and their critical echoes are united. "He wrote some later novels of indifferent merit," says a gentleman in *Chambers' Encyclopædia*. "Has any one ever been able to write with free and genuine appreciation of even the later novels?" echoes the voice of a lady, Miss Grace Toplis,

"AMARYLLIS AT THE FAIR"

writing on Jefferies. " In brief, he was an essayist and not a novelist at all," says Mr. Henry Salt. " It is therefore certain that his importance for posterity will dwindle, if it has not already dwindled, to that given by a bundle of descriptive selections. But these will occupy a foremost place on their particular shelf, the shelf at the head of which stand Gilbert White and Gray," says Mr. George Saintsbury. " He was a reporter of genius, and he never got beyond reporting. Mr. Besant has the vitalising imagination which Jefferies lacked," says Mr. Henley in his review of Walter Besant's *Eulogy of Richard Jefferies*; and again, " They are not novels as he (Walter Besant) admits, they are a series of pictures. . . . That is the way he takes Jefferies at Jefferies' worst." Yes, it is very touching this unanimity, and it is therefore a pleasure for this critic to say that in his judgment *Amaryllis at the Fair* is one of the very few later-day novels of English country life that are worth putting on one's shelf, and that to make room for it he would turn out certain highly-praised novels by Hardy which do not ring quite true, novels which the critics and the public, again with touching unanimity, have voted to be of high rank. But what is a novel? the reader may ask. A novel, says the learned Professor Annandale, is " a fictitious prose narrative, involving some plot of greater or less intricacy, and professing to give a picture of real life, generally exhibiting the passions and sentiments in a state of great activity, and especially the passion of love." Well, *Amaryllis at the Fair* is a fictitious prose narrative professing to give a picture of real life, and involving a plot of little intricacy. Certainly it exhibits the passions and sentiments in a state of great activity. But Mr Henry Salt, whose little book on Jefferies is the best yet published, further remarks: "Jefferies was quite unable to give any vivid dramatic life to his stories . . . his instinct was that of the naturalist who observes and moralises rather than that of the novelist who penetrates and interprets; and consequently his rustic characters, though strongly and clearly drawn, do not live, as, for example, those of Thomas Hardy live. . . . Men and animals are alike mere figures in his landscapes."

So far the critics. Jefferies being justly held to be "no ordinary novelist," it is inferred by most that something is wrong with *Amaryllis at the Fair*, and the book is passed over in silence. But we do not judge every novel by the same test. We do not judge *Tristram Shandy*, for example, by its intricate plot, or by its "vivid drama," we judge it simply as an artistic revelation of human life and by its humorous insight into human character. And judged by the same simple test *Amaryllis at the Fair*, we contend, is a living picture of life, a creative work of imagination of a high order. Iden, the unsuccessful farmer who "built for all time, and not for the circumstances of the hour," is a masterly piece of character drawing. But Iden is a personal portrait, the reader may object. Well, what about

"AMARYLLIS AT THE FAIR"

Uncle Toby? From what void did he spring? Iden, to our mind, is almost as masterly a conception, as broadly human a figure as Uncle Toby. And Mrs. Iden, where will you find this type of nervous, irritable wife, full of spiteful disillusioned love for her dilatory husband, better painted than by Jefferies? But Mrs. Iden is a type, not an individual, the reader may say. Excellent reader! and what about the Widow Wadman? She is no less and no more of an individual than is Mrs. Iden. It was a great feat of Sterne to create so cunningly the atmosphere of the Shandy household, but Jefferies has accomplished an artistic feat also in drawing the relations of the Idens, father, mother, and daughter. How true, how unerringly true to human nature is this picture of the Iden household; how delicately felt and rendered to a hair is his picture of the father's sluggish, masculine will, pricked ineffectually by the waspish tongue of feminine criticism. Further, we not only have the family's idiosyncrasies, their habits, mental atmosphere, and domestic story brought before us in a hundred pages, easily and instinctively by the hand of the artist, but we have the whole book steeped in the breath of English spring, the restless ache of spring that thrills through the nerves, and stirs the sluggish winter blood; we have the spring feeling breaking from the March heavens, and the March earth in copse, meadow, and ploughland as it has scarcely been rendered before by English novelist. The description of Amaryllis running out into the March wind to call her father from his potato planting to see the daffodil; the picture of Iden pretending to sleep in his chair that he may watch the mice; the description of the girl Amaryllis watching the crowd of plain, ugly men of the countryside flocking along the road to the fair; the description of Amadis the invalid, in the old farm kitchen among the stalwart country folk—all these pictures and a dozen others in the book are painted with a masterly hand. Pictures! the critical reader may complain. Yes, pictures of living men and women. What does it matter whether a revelation of human life is conveyed to us by pictures or by action so long as it is conveyed? Mr. Saintsbury classes Jefferies with Gray, presumably because both writers have written of the English landscape. With Gray! Jefferies in his work as a naturalist and observer of wild life may be classed merely for convenience with Gilbert White. But this classification only applies to one half of Jefferies' books. By his *Wild Life in a Southern County* he stands beside Gilbert White; by his *Story of My Heart* he stands by himself, a little apart from the poets, and by *Amaryllis at the Fair* he stands among the half-dozen country writers of the century whose work is racy of the English soil and of rural English human nature. I will name three of these writers, Barnes, Cobbett, Waugh, and my attentive readers can name the other three.

To come back to *Amaryllis at the Fair*, why is

it so masterly, or, further, wherein is it so masterly, the curious reader may inquire? " Is it not full of digressions? Granted that the first half of the 'novel' is beautiful in style, does not Jefferies suddenly break his method, introduce his own personality, intersperse abrupt disquisitions on food, illness, and Fleet Street? Is not that description of Iden's dinner a little—well, a little unusual? In short, is not the book a disquisition on life from the standpoint of Jefferies' personal experiences? And if this is so, how can the book be so fine an achievement?" Oh, candid reader, with the voice of authority sounding in your ears (and have we not Messrs. Henley, Saintsbury and Toplis bound in critical amity against us?) a book may break the formal rules, and yet it may yield to us just that salt of life which we may seek for vainly in the works of more faultless writers. The strength of *Amaryllis at the Fair* is that its beauty springs naturally from the prosaic earthly facts of life it narrates, and that, in the natural atmosphere breathed by its people, the prose and the poetry of their life are one. In respect of the artistic naturalness of its homely picture, the book is very superior to, say *The Mayor of Casterbridge*, where we are conscious that the author has been at work arranging and rearranging his charming studies and impressions of the old-world people of Casterbridge into the pattern of an exciting plot. Now it is precisely in the artificed dramatic story of *The Mayor of Casterbridge*— and we cite this novel as characteristic both in its strength and weakness of its distinguished author —that we are brought to feel that we have not been shown the characters of Casterbridge going their way in life naturally, but that they have been moved about, kaleidoscopically, to suit the exigencies of the plot, and that the more this is done the less significance for us have their thoughts and actions. Watching the quick whirling changes of Farfrae and Lucetta, Henchard and Newson in the matrimonial mazes of the story, we perceive indeed whence comes that atmosphere of stage crisis and stage effect which suddenly introduces a disillusioning sense of unreality, and mars the artistic unity of this charming picture, so truthful in other respects to Wessex rural life. Plot is Mr. Hardy's weakness, and perfect indeed and convincing would have been his pictures if he could have thrown his plots to the four winds. May we not be thankful, therefore, that Jefferies was no hand at elaborating a plot, and that in *Amaryllis at the Fair*, the scenes, the descriptions, the conversations are spontaneous as life, and Jefferies' commentary on them is like Fielding's commentary, a medium by which he lives with his characters. The author's imagination, memory, and instinctive perception are all working together. And thus his picture of country life in *Amaryllis* brings with it as convincing and as fresh a breath of life as we find in Cobbett's, Waugh's and Barnes' country writings. When a writer arrives at being perfectly natural in his atmosphere, his style and his subject seem to become one. He moves easily and surely. Out of the splintered mass of ideas and emotions, out of the sensations, the observations and revelations of his youth, and the atmosphere familiar to him through long feeling, he builds up a subtle and cunning picture for us, a complete illusion of life more true than the reality. For what prosaic people call the reality is merely the co-ordination in their own minds of perhaps a hundredth part of the aspects of life around them; and only this hundredth part they have noticed. But the creative mind builds up a living picture out of the hundreds of aspects most of us are congenitally blind to. This is what Jefferies has done in *Amaryllis at the Fair*. The book is rich in the contradictory forces of life, in its quick twists and turns: we feel in it there is nature working alike in the leaves of grass outside the Idens' house, in the blustering winds round the walls, and in the minds of the characters indoors; and the style is as fresh as the April wind. Everything is growing, changing, breathing in the book. But the accomplished critics do not notice these trivial strengths! It is enough for them that Jefferies was not a novelist! Indeed, Mr. Saintsbury apparently thinks that Jefferies made a mistake in drawing his philosophy from an open-air study of nature, for he writes: "Unfortunately for Jefferies his philosophic background was not like Wordsworth's, clear and cheerful, but wholly vague and partly gloomy." It was neither vague nor gloomy, we may remark, parenthetically, but we may admit that Jefferies saw too directly Nature's life to interpret all Nature's doings, *à la* Wordsworth, and lend them a philosophic, solemn significance.

The one charge that may with truth be brought against *Amaryllis at the Fair* is that its digressions damage the artistic illusion of the whole. The book shows the carelessness, the haste, the roughness of a sketch, a sketch, moreover, which Jefferies was not destined to carry to the end he had planned; but we repeat, let us be thankful that its artistic weaknesses are those of a sketch direct from nature, rather than those of an ambitious studio picture. But these digressions are an integral part of the book's character, just as the face of a man has its own blemishes: they are one with the spirit of the whole, and so, if they break somewhat the illusion of the scenes, they do not damage its spiritual unity. It is this spiritual unity on which we must insist, because *Amaryllis* is indeed Jefferies' last and complete testament on human life. He wrote it, or rather dictated it to his wife, as he lay in pain, slowly dying, and he has put into it the frankness of a dying man. How real, how solid, how deliciously sweet seemed those simple earthly joys, those human appetites of healthy, vigorous men to him! How intense is his passion and spiritual hunger for the beauty of earth! Like a flame shooting up from the log it is consuming, so this passion for the green earth, for the earth in wind and rain and sunshine, consumes the wasted, con-

"AMARYLLIS AT THE FAIR"

sumptive body of the dying man. The reality, the solidity of the homely farm-house life he describes spring from the intensity with which he clings to all he loves, to the cold March wind buffeting the face, the mating cries of the birds in the hot sunshine. Life is so terribly strong, so deliciously real, so full of man's unsatisfied hungry ache for happiness; and sweet is the craving, bitter the knowledge of the unfulfilment. So, inspiring and vivifying the whole, in every line of *Amaryllis* is Jefferies' philosophy of life. Jefferies " did not understand human nature," say the learned, the erudite critics. Did he not ? *Amaryllis at the Fair* is one of the truest criticisms of human life, oh reader, you are likely to meet with. The mixedness of things, the old, old human muddle, the meanness and stupidity and shortsightedness of humanity, the good salty taste of life in the healthy mouth, the spirituality of love, the strong earthy roots of appetite, man's lust of life, with circumstances awry, and the sharp wind blowing alike on the just and the unjust— all is there on the printed page of *Amaryllis at the Fair*. The song of the wind and the roar of London unite and mingle therein for those who do not bring the exacting eye of superiority to this most human book.

THE POETRY OF JOHN CLARE

By J. Middleton Murry

In 1820 Messrs. Taylor and Hessey published two books whose immediate renown was in singular contrast with their after-fame. *Poems Descriptive of Rural Life and Scenery*, by John Clare, a Northamptonshire Peasant, ran into four editions within a year; the five hundred copies of the single edition, *Lamia, Isabella, and other Poems*, by John Keats, were not exhausted till the 'forties. Clare's popularity dwindled gradually into complete neglect; he had been all but wholly forgotten by the time that Monckton Milnes assumed the practical task of impressing upon the world the conviction of the poets that Keats was among the greatest. Quickly the labours of piety were accomplished; within a few years Keats's poetical remains were gathered together, until nothing substantial remained to be added. Clare went on writing indefatigably in the exile of an asylum for nearly thirty years after he had been forgotten, and not till to-day have two young poets set themselves to the task of rescuing all that is valuable in his work.[1]

[1] *John Clare: Poems.* Chiefly from Manuscript. Selected and Edited by Edmund Blunden and Alan Porter.

THE POETRY OF JOHN CLARE

It is not merely because the year and the publishers were the same that we are drawn to think of Keats and Clare together. The association of the great name and the small one has a curious congruity. Keats and Clare both suffered "a vast shipwreck of their life's esteems," the one sudden and intolerably tragic, the other lingering and not without a sunset-haze of vaguely remembered happiness. There were elements common to their characters — they were both parvenus in the ranks of men of letters, and they shared a resolution and an independence which became almost intolerant; Keats had an unusual, and Clare a unique knowledge of country sights and sounds; the most perfect poem of each is an *Ode to Autumn.*

We are inclined to lay stress on the points of resemblance in order that the cardinal point of difference may more plainly appear; for the eagerness with which we welcome this collection of Clare's poetry is likely to be so genuine and so justified as to disturb our sense of proportion. Into a generation of poets who flirt with nature suddenly descends a true nature-poet, one whose intimate and self-forgetful knowledge of the ways of birds and beasts and flowers rises like the scent of open fields from every page. Surely the only danger is that the enthusiasm of our recognition may be excessive; the relief overpowering with which we greet a poet who not only professes, but proves by the very words of his profession, that his dream of delight is

> To note on hedgerow baulks, in moisture sprent
> The jetty snail creep from the mossy thorn,
> With earnest heed and tremulous intent,
> Frail brother of the morn,
> That from the tiny bents and misted leaves
> Withdraws his timid horn,
> And fearful vision weaves.

We have indeed almost to be on our guard against the sweet, cool shock of such a verse; the emotional quality is so assured and individual, the language so simple and inevitable, the posture of mind so unassuming and winning, that one is tempted for a moment to believe that while Wordsworth was engaged in putting the poetry of nature wrong by linking it to a doubtful metaphysic, John Clare was engaged in putting it right.

And so in a sense it was. As a poet of nature Clare was truer, more thoroughly subdued to that in which he worked than Wordsworth. Wordsworth called upon the poet to keep his eye upon the object; but his eye was hardly so penetrating and keen as Clare's. Yet Wordsworth was a great poet, and Keats, with whom Clare's kinship was really closer, was a great poet, and Clare was not; and it is important in the case of a poet whose gifts and qualities are so enchanting as Clare's are to bear in mind from the outset the vital difference between them. Wordsworth belongs to another sphere than Clare in virtue of the range of his imaginative apprehension; Keats in virtue not only of his imagination,

THE POETRY OF JOHN CLARE

but also of his art. In one respect Clare was a finer artist than Wordsworth, he had a truer ear and a more exquisite instinct for words; but he had nothing of the principle of inward growth which gives to Wordsworth's most careless work a place within the unity of a great scheme. Wordsworth's incessant effort to comprehend experience would itself have been incomprehensible to Clare; Keats's consuming passion to make his poetry adequate not merely in content but also in the very mechanism of expression to an emotional experience more overwhelming even than Wordsworth's would have been like a problem of metaphysics to a ploughboy.

Clare was indeed a singer born. His nature was strangely simple, and his capacity for intense emotion appears at first sight to have been almost completely restricted to a reaction to nature. The intensity with which he adored the country which he knew is without a parallel in English literature; of him it seems hardly a metaphor to say he was an actual part of his countryside. Away from it he pined; he became queer and irresponsible. With his plants and birds and bees and fields he was among his own people. The spiked thistle, the firetail, the hare, the white-nosed and the grandfather bee were his friends. Yet he hardly humanised them; he seems rather to have lived on the same level of existence as they, and to have known them as they know each other. We feel that it is only by an effort that he manages to make himself conscious of his emotion towards them or of his own motive in singing of it. In those rare moments he conceives of the voice of Nature as something eternal, outlasting all generations of men, whispering to them to sing also. Thus, while he sits under the huge old elm which is the shepherd's tree, listening to " the laugh of summer leaves above,"

> The wind of that eternal ditty sings,
> Humming of future things that burn the mind
> To leave some fragment of itself behind.

That is the most imaginative statement Clare ever made of his own poetic purpose. He, the poet, is one more of Nature's voices; and the same thought or the same instinct underlies the most exquisite of his earlier poems, *Song's Eternity*, a precious discovery of his present editors:

> Mighty songs that miss decay,
>   What are they?
> Crowds and cities pass away
>   Like a day.
> Books are out and books are read;
>   What are they?
> Years will lay them with the dead—
>   Sigh, sigh;
> Trifles unto nothing wed,
>   They die.
>
> Dreamers, mark the honey bee,
>   Mark the tree
> Where the bluecap *tootle-tee*
>   Sings a glee
> Sung to Adam and to Eve—
>   Here they be.
> When floods covered every bough
>   Noah's ark
> Heard that ballad singing now;
>   Hark, hark,

THE POETRY OF JOHN CLARE

Tootle tootle tootle tee.
   Can it be
Pride and fame must shadows be?
   Come and see—
Every season own her own;
   Bird and bee
Sing creation's music on;
   Nature's glee
Is in every mood and tone
   Eternity.

In many ways that is the most perfect of Clare's poems; it has a poetic unity of a kind that he attained but seldom, for in it are naturally combined the highest apprehension of which Clare was capable and the essential melody of his pre-eminent gift of song. It is at once an assertion and an emotional proof of the enduringness of the voice of Nature. Clare does not, like the modern poet who has chosen the same theme, adduce the times and the seasons and thereby challenge the evolutionary theory; his history is the history of myth. Not the Neanderthal man but Adam and Eve heard the bluecap's same, immortal song; for it is not the fact, but the sense of song's eternity that the poet has to give us. Clare does it triumphantly. Moreover, in this poem, which we believe must henceforward take its place by right in every anthology of English poetry, Clare achieved that final perfection of form which was so often to elude him. The bird-note begins, rises, dies away: and the poem is finished.

   Clare's music was a natural music; as with Shelley's skylark, his art was unpremeditated and his strains profuse. He was perhaps never to find a form which fitted his genius so intimately as that of *Song's Eternity*. His language was to become more coherent and more vivid; but the inward harmony that is essential to a great poem was too often to escape him. He was like a child so intoxicated with his wonderful gift for whistling and his tune that he whistles it over and over again. The note is so pure, the tune so full of delight that we can never be tired; we listen to it as we listen to the drowsy enchantment of the monotony of sounds on a summer's afternoon, for it is as authentic and as sweet as they. The eternity of song was in Clare's blood; and when he recurs to the theme of enduring nature in simple stanzas,

> Some sing the pomps of chivalry
>   As legends of the ancient time,
> Where gold and pearls and mystery
>   Are shadows painted for sublime;
>
> But passions of sublimity
>   Belong to plain and simpler things,
> And David underneath a tree
>   Sought when a shepherd Salem's springs,
>
> Where moss did into cushions spring,
>   Forming a seat of velvet hue,
> A small unnoticed trifling thing
>   To all but heaven's hailing dew.
>
> And David's crown hath passed away,
>   Yet poesy breathes his shepherd skill,
> His palace lost—and to this day
>   The little moss is blossoming still.

we feel that here, too, is a music that need never end.

THE POETRY OF JOHN CLARE

Clare's difficulty as a poet, in fact, can and ought to be put baldly; he did not know when to stop. Why, indeed, should he stop? He was either a voice, one of the unending voices of Nature, or he was an eye, an unwearied eye watching the infinite process of Nature; perhaps never a poet consciously striving by means of art to arouse in men's minds an emotion like his own. All the art he had was that which he gained from his recollection of other poets' tunes; the structure of their harmony eluded him, he remembered only the melody. Take, for instance, his extremely beautiful *Autumn*: the melody comes directly from Collins's famous Ode; yet how greatly Clare enriches it, as though with a material golden stain of autumn! The last leaf seems to be falling at our feet, the last bee zooming in our ears.

> Heart-sickening for the silence that is thine,
> Not broken inharmoniously as now
>   That lone and vagrant bee
>   Booms faint with weary chime.
>
> Now filtering winds thin winnow through the woods
> In tremulous noise that bids at every breath
>   Some sickly cankered leaf
>   Let go its hold, and die.

Not only these, but any one of a dozen other stanzas in the poem have a richer mellowness, reveal a finer sensitiveness than any in Collins's lovely Ode. For all that the melody derives from Collins, we are borne away from him to the neighbourhood of Keats's great poem. But Collins had a classical, almost Miltonic, sense of form; what he lacked in the richness of direct perception he supplied by his careful concentration of emotional effect: so that, despite the more splendid beauty of the elements of Clare's poem, we dare not say it is really finer than Collins's Ode. Collins gathers up all his more exiguous perceptions into a single stimulus to emotion: Clare lets them fall one by one, careless of his amazing jewels. Set his *Autumn* against Keats's three verses, where the imagination has come to crystallise perceptions not less rich in themselves than Clare's into a single symbol—the very spirit of Autumn.

> Who hath not seen thee oft amid thy store?
>   Sometimes whoever seeks abroad may find
> Thee sitting careless on a granary floor
>   Thy hair soft lifted by the winnowing wind;
> Or on a half-reaped furrow sound asleep
>   Drowsed with the fume of poppies, while thy hook
> Spares the next swathe and all its twined flowers;
> And sometimes like a gleaner thou dost keep
>   Steady thy laden head across a brook
>   Or by a cyder-press, with patient look,
> Thou watchest the last oozings hours by hours.

Clare could not do that; for Keats had Collins's art and Clare's richness of perception, and he had also that incomparable imaginative power which alone can create the perfect symbol of an overwhelming and intricate emotion.

Yet we need to invoke Keats to explain Clare, and to understand fully why his wealth of perception was refined into so few perfect poems. Collins himself is not sufficient for the purpose; one cannot well invoke the success of a poorer to explain the failure of a richer nature. Keats the great poetic artist, however, subsumes Clare. Careless critics, confusing the life of every day with the life of the poetic mind, rebuke Keats for his lack of discipline. Yet where in English poetry shall we find a power of poetic discipline greater than his, a more determined and inevitable compulsion of the whole of a poet's emotional experience into the single symbol, the one organic and inevitable form? In him were combined miraculously the humanity that can reject no element of true experience and the artistic integrity to which less than a complete mastery and transformation of experience is intolerable. When, therefore, we invoke Keats to explain Clare, when we feel the need to merge Clare into Keats in thought in order that we may discover his own poetic fulfilment, by completing the great pattern of which he is a fragment, we are passing a judgment upon the value and quality of Clare's own work of which the implications are unescapable. It is a fragment, but it is a fragment of the Parthenon pediment, of intrinsic value, unique, and beyond price.

Clare's qualities were authentic and without alloy. It was the power to refine and shape his metal that was denied him; his workshop is littered not with dross but with veritable gold—of melody, of an intensity of perception (truly, his "mind was burned"), and, more rarely, of flashes of that passion of the pure imagination which is the mysterious source of the magic of poetry. Let our partial quotation of *Song's Eternity* suffice to prove the quality of his spontaneous melody. For the intensity of perception we may choose at random any page in this book. Is not a picture such as this cast upon " that inward eye " ?

> Where squats the hare to terrors wide awake
> Like some brown clod the harrows failed to break.

Such things are scattered throughout Clare; they range from the quiet vision of the actual, focussed by a single word, such as

> The old pond with its water-weed
> And danger-daring willow-tree,
> Who leans, an ancient invalid,
> O'er spots where deepest waters be,

to the authentic fancy of

> Here morning in the ploughman's songs is met
> Ere yet one footstep shows in all the sky,
> And twilight in the East, a doubt as yet,
> Shows not her sleeve of gray to know her by.

How perfect is the image, as perfect to its context and emotion as the " sovran eye " of Shakespeare's sun! And what of the intense compression of a phrase like " ploughed lands thin travelled by half-hungry sheep," precise not merely to a fact, but to an emotion ?

This unmistakable core of pure emotion lies close to the surface throughout Clare. His precision is the precision of a lover; he watches nature as a man might watch his mistress's eyes; his breath is bated, and we seem to hear the very thumping of his heart; and there are moments when the emotion seems to rise in a sudden fountain and change the thing he sees into a jewel. "Frail brother of the morn" to a jetty snail is the tender cry of a passionate lover; there is a delicateness in the emotion expressed which not even Wordsworth could attain when he called upon the Lesser Celandine. It is love of this kind that gives true significance to the poetry of nature, for only by its alchemy can the thing seen become the symbol of the thing felt: washed by the magic tide of an overwhelming emotion, the object shines with a pure and lucid radiance, transformed from a cause to a symbol of delight, and thus no longer delighting the senses and the emotions alone, but the mind. This mysterious faculty is not indeed the highest kind of poetic imagination, in which the intellect plays a greater part in the creation of the symbol; this emotional creation leaps from particular to particular, it lacks that endorsement from a centre of disciplined experience which is the mark of the poetic imagination at its highest: but it is purely poetic and truly creative.

In this authentic kind Clare was all but a master, and it may even be suspected that his unique gift would have suffered if he had possessed that element of technical control which would have made him a master indeed. For when we come to define as narrowly as we can the distinctive, compelling quality of his emotion, we find that in addition to tenderness we need the word impulsive. Clare's most beautiful poetry is a gesture of impulsive tenderness. It has a curious suddenness, almost a catch in the voice.

> The very darkness smiles to wear
> The stars that show us God is there.

We find, too, a still more authentic mark of the tenderness of impulsive love in his way of seeing his birds and beasts as ever so little absurd. "Absurd" has a peculiar and delightful meaning in the converse of lovers; Clare's firetail is "absurd" in precisely the same sense.

> Of everything that stirs she dreameth wrong,
> And pipes her " tweet-tut " fears the whole day long.

And so, too, are his bees—the "grandfather bee," the wild bees who "with their legs stroke slumber from their eyes," "the little bees with coal-black faces, gathering sweets from little flowers like stars"; even the riddle of the quail appears to be rather a delicate and lovable waywardness in the bird than a mere ignorance in the man.

> Among the stranger birds they feed,
> Their summer flight is short and low;
> There's very few know where they breed
> And scarcely any where they go.

A tenderness of this exquisite and impulsive kind might have been damaged as much as strengthened by a firmer technical control; a shiver of constraint might have crept into the gesture itself and chilled it; and perhaps we may touch the essential nature

THE POETRY OF JOHN CLARE

of Clare's emotion most closely in the mysterious and haunting Asylum poem, discovered by the present editors, and called by them *Secret Love*.

> I hid my love when young till I
> Couldn't bear the buzzing of a fly;
> I hid my love to my despite
> Till I could not bear to look at light;
> I dare not gaze upon her face
> But left her memory in each place;
> Where'er I saw a wild flower lie
> I kissed and bade my love good-bye.
>
> I met her in the greenest dells
> Where dewdrops pearl the wood blue bells,
> The lost breeze kissed her bright blue eye,
> The bee kissed and went singing by;
> A sunbeam found a passage there,
> A gold chain round her neck so fair;
> As secret as the wild bee's song
> She lay there all the summer long.
>
> I hid my love in field and town
> Till e'en the breeze would knock me down,
> The bees seemed singing ballads o'er,
> The fly's bass turned a lion's roar;
> And even silence found a tongue
> To haunt me all the summer long;
> The riddle nature could not prove
> Was nothing else but secret love.

Clare is invoking the memory of Mary Joyce, the girl lover whom he did not marry, and who, though long since dead, lived for him as his true wife when he was immured in the asylum. But the fact of this strange passion is less remarkable than its precise quality; it is an intolerable tenderness, an unbearable surge of emotion eager to burst forth and lavish itself upon an object. Whether it was his passion for Mary Joyce which first awakened him to an awareness of the troublous depths of emotion within we cannot tell, for this poem is in itself no evidence of fact. But it bears witness unmistakable to the quality of the emotion which underlay all that is characteristic and unforgettable in his poetry.

When we have touched the unique emotional core which persists throughout the work of a true poet, we have come perhaps as near as we can to his secret. We stand as it were at the very source of his creation. In the great poetic artist we may follow out the intricacies and ramifications of the intellectual structure by which he makes the expression of his central emotion complete, and the emotion itself permanent. In Clare the work is unnecessary. The emotion is hardly mediated at all. The poetic creation is instinctive and impulsive; the love is poured out, and the bird, the beast, the flower is made glorious. It is the very process which Stendhal described, with fitting brilliancy, as *la cristallisation de l'amour*.

We may therefore most truly describe Clare as the love poet of nature; and we need not pause to explore the causes why nature and not a human being was turned to crystal by the magical process of his love. Those who care to know may find the story woven in among the narrative of Mr. Blunden's sympathetic introduction; they can discover for themselves the reason why Clare appears in the world of grown men and women as a stranger

THE POETRY OF JOHN CLARE

and a changeling; why the woman of his dreams is disembodied; why, when he calls to her in his *Invitation to Eternity*, the present is " marred with reason ":

> The land of shadows wilt thou trace
> Nor look nor know each other's face;
> The present marred with reason gone
> And past and present both as one?
> Say, maiden, can thy life be led
> To join the living and the dead?
> Then trace thy footsteps on with me:
> We are wed to one eternity.

In eternity perhaps a woman, but in the actual Nature was Clare's mistress; her he served and cherished with a tenderness and faithful knowledge unique in the poetry of nature. Like a true lover he stammered in long speeches, but he spoke to her the divinest and most intimate things. Assuredly his lines were cast so that he had no need of woman even in eternity, and perhaps the truest words he ever wrote of himself are those of the poem by which he is most generally known:

> I long for scenes where man has never trod;
>   A place where woman never smiled nor wept;
> There to abide with my creator, God,
>   And sleep as I in childhood sweetly slept:
> Untroubling and untroubled where I lie;
> The grass below—above the vaulted sky.

ON GOING DRY
By A. A. Milne

THERE are fortunate mortals who can always comfort themselves with a cliché. If any question arises as to the moral value of Racing, whether in war-time or in peace-time, they will murmur something about "improving the breed of horses," and sleep afterwards with an easy conscience. To one who considers how many millions of people are engaged upon this important work, it is surprising that nothing more notable in the way of a super-horse has as yet emerged; one would have expected at least by this time something which combined the flying-powers of the hawk with the diving-powers of the seal. No doubt this is what the followers of the Colonel's Late Wire are aiming at, and even if they have to borrow ten shillings from the till in the good cause, they feel that possibly by means of that very ten shillings Nature has approximated a little more closely to the desired animal. Supporters of Hunting, again, will tell you, speaking from inside knowledge, that "the fox likes it," and one is left breathless at the thought of the altruism of the human race, which will devote so much time and money to amusing a small, bushy-tailed four-legged friend who might otherwise be bored. And the third member of the Triple Alliance, which has made England what it is, is Beer, and in support of Beer there is also a cliché ready. Talk to anybody about Intemperance, and he will tell you solemnly, as if this disposed of the trouble, that " one can just as easily be intemperate in other matters as in the matter of alcohol." After which, it seems almost a duty to a broad-minded man to go out and get drunk.

It is, of course, true that we can be intemperate in eating as well as in drinking, but the results of the intemperance would appear to be different. After a fifth help of rice-pudding one does not become over-familiar with strangers, nor does an extra slice of ham inspire a man to beat his wife. After five pints of beer (or fifteen, or fifty) a man will " go anywhere in reason, but he won't go home "; after five helps of rice-pudding, I imagine, home would seem to him the one-desired haven. The two intemperances may be equally blameworthy, but they are not equally offensive to the community. Yet for some reason over-eating is considered the mark of the beast, and over-drinking the mark of rather a fine fellow.

The poets and other gentlemen who have written so much romantic nonsense about " good red wine " and " good brown ale " are responsible for this. I admit that a glass of Burgundy is a more beautiful thing than a blancmange, but I do not think that it follows that a surfeit of one is more heroic than a surfeit of the other. There may be a divinity in the grape which excuses excess, but if so, one would expect it to be there even before the grape had been trodden on by somebody else. Yet no poet ever hymned the man who tucked into the dessert, or told him that he was by way of becoming a jolly good fellow. He is only by way of becoming a pig.

"It is the true, the blushful Hippocrene." To tell oneself this is to pardon everything. However unpleasant a drunken man may seem at first sight, as soon as one realises that he has merely been putting away a blushful Hippocrene, one ceases to be angry with him. If Keats or somebody had said of a piece of underdone mutton, "It is the true, the blushful Canterbury," indigestion would carry a more romantic air, and at the third helping one could claim to be a bit of a devil. "The beaded bubbles winking at the brim"—this might also have been sung of a tapioca-pudding, in which case a couple of tapioca-puddings would certainly qualify the recipient as one of the boys. If only the poets had praised over-eating rather than over-drinking, how much pleasanter the streets would be on festival nights!

I suppose that I have already said enough to have written myself down a Temperance Fanatic, a Thin-Blooded Cocoa-Drinker, and a number of other things equally contemptible; which is all very embarrassing to a man who is composing at the moment on port, and who gets entangled in the skin of cocoa whenever he tries to approach it. But if anything could make me take kindly to cocoa, it would be the sentimental rubbish which is written about the "manliness" of drinking alcohol. It is no more manly to drink beer (not even if you call it good brown ale) than it is to drink beef-tea. It may be more healthy; I know nothing about that, nor, from the diversity of opinion expressed, do the doctors; it may be cheaper, more thirst-quenching, anything you like. But it is a thing the village idiot can do—and often does, without becoming thereby the spiritual comrade of Robin Hood, King Harry the Fifth, Drake, and all the other heroes who (if we are to believe the Swill School) have made old England great on beer.

But to doubt the spiritual virtues of alcohol is not to be a Prohibitionist. For my own sake I want neither England nor America dry. Whether I want them dry for the sake of England and America I cannot quite decide. But if I ever do come to a decision, it will not be influenced by that other cliché, which is often trotted out complacently, as if it were something to thank Heaven for: "You can't make people moral by Act of Parliament." It is not a question of making them moral, but of keeping them from alcohol. It may be a pity to do this, but it is obviously possible, just as it is possible to keep them—that is to say, the overwhelming majority of them—from opium. Nor shall I be influenced by the argument that such prohibition is outside the authority of a Government. For if a Government can demand a man's life for reasons of foreign policy, it can surely demand his whisky for reasons of domestic policy; if it can call upon him to start fighting, it can call upon him to stop drinking.

But if opium and alcohol are prohibited, you say, why not tobacco? When tobacco is mentioned, I feel like the village Socialist, who was quite ready to share two theoretical cows with his neighbour, but when asked if the theory applied also to pigs, answered indignantly, "What are you talking about—I've *got* two pigs!" I could bear an England which "went dry," but an England which "went out"——! So before assenting to the right of a Government to rob the workingman of his beer, I have to ask myself if I assent to its right to rob me of my pipe. Well, if it were agreed by a majority of the community (in spite of all my hymns to Nicotine) that England would be happier without tobacco, then I think I should agree also. But I might feel that I should be happier without England. Just a little way without—the Isle of Man, say.

THE VENICE OF ENGLAND
By H. J. Massingham

Than Blakeney on the north coast of Norfolk there is no lonelier place in England, so lone and level that the sun vaults over it in one majestic sweep from east to west, like a grasshopper bounding over a strip of lawn. Under the cupola of the heavens the eye rests on nothing but a hut or an old hulk stranded in the mud of the tidal creeks, and they are stars in a void the emptier for them, while sky and land and sea are interpenetrated each with the other, mingling their essences in a partnership of Titan substance which seems to be designing the birth of new worlds. And elemental birth there is, for these calm solitudes are the theatre of an intense energy condensed into a speck of geological time, a grandiose parade and strife of forces, a procreant urge, a crest and subsidence of being that lay the ferment of creation bare to our wonder.

Blakeney Point is a narrow tongue of land built up of the three great systems of the shore, sand dune, shingle beach and salting, running parallel with the tidal marshes of the mainland and separated from it by an estuary which at low tide is a river and at high an inland sea. Within this area clash the powers of land and sea. The sea rolls in its regiments of shingle, depositing petrified waves of it in parallel humps and furrows, fosses and ramparts against its own advance: the shingle creeps upon the land, but the *Pelvetia* seaweed and the *Suæda* bushes wave their fronds upon its crests, arresting and scooping it about the matted filaments with which they clench the stones; the sea flings out its flying squadrons of sand and the wiry marram grass holds it tight and presses it into the service of life-giving soil, throwing up a range of sandhills in ten years, while the parallel ranges behind shrink as the wind bears down upon them and scatters their grains away; the columns of the waves charge upon the land and leave in their tidal drift the seeds of plants which garment sand and stone with living greens and greys. The earth in its turn casts the spray of its teeming growth into the sea's challenge, some of it—hawkweed, dock, plantain, crowfoot, stonecrop, mayweed, catchfly and bird's-foot trefoil—mindful of their ancient home; others—glaucous sea-purslane, sea-lavender, sea-aster, samphire, sea-rocket, the oyster-plant with its delicate blue flower and the polymorphic sea-campion with its seven varieties, some with lobed petals, others incurved—adopted of the sea and the flowers of its garden. There is no element, process nor growth here that does not take from and give to its fellows, that, ever restless, mobile and unstable, does not image in every stage of development and decay the heave and tumble of the waves that travel in from the Pole.

THE VENICE OF ENGLAND

And the colours of Blakeney, the Venice of England, if, as Dr. Oliver says, Venice be not the Blakeney of Italy, are truly the sparks and flares of the elemental factory. The land moves not only in the mirage of the heat-haze's undulating light; the silver-grey foliage of the sea-purslane shifting to pink through the young leaves, like a young hare's transparent ear, and to lavender in the shadows, is a tiny reflection of the huge mobility of colour in the full landscape. The ultramarine of sky paling to turquoise on the horizon, of the sea shot like silk with green; the metallic emerald of the algæ on the mud-flats; the umber of the sandhills; the yellows, oranges, greens and whites of the flowers; the pearls of the shells sewn like jewels into the shingle-pelt, exchange their glowing robes every minute according to the drying of the ground and the density of vapour in different places, and in their flushing or pallor, with all the grades of tone between, seem to dramatise in their medium all the moods of passionate life, of becoming, of being and of dying.

Of this creative power and vehemence, seen in its very discharge, the terns are the perfect art and expression. They are the absolute of bird-life in the sense that their inhuman loveliness, though the most highly finished of that of any bird known to me, is yet elemental, making one reflect that in evolution we do not get rid of the elemental, but see further into it. They are elemental in Nature's world, as Blake is in ours, the elysian flower of the tough roots of things, so fair, free and frail that they might well be the substance, hovering on the border between sense and spirit, of wind, wave and "argentine vapour." If they were souls, they would yet enjoy the earth; if creatures of flesh, theirs too an immaterial world. The experience of walking among their airy legions in the full breeding season is one of the richest and strangest. At Blakeney Point and on the Salt-house marches at its heel some four thousand of them were nesting in 1922 among black-headed gulls, oyster-catchers, ringed plover, sheld-duck and redshank, five species in all, the Common, the Arctic, the Sandwich, the Little and the Roseate Tern, the last (one pair) faint-blushed with rose beneath for the dazzling white of the Sandwich and the pearls of the others, with longer streamers and even finer build, carrying tern-structure to the extremest point of art in delicacy of line and shape. A little more, one feels, and this rarest being would be resolved back into mist and spray.

Nor is he far from them, for the plumage trader and the collector have so reduced the number that the remnant find it hard to keep a foothold among the multitude of their brethren. They show the same nicety of differentiation in other directions, the Sandwich being as large in proportion to the Common and Arctic Terns as the Little Tern is small, more wavering on the wing, and with a crescent of white between the bill and the black cap, which so precisely adjusts and focuses in them all the relations of the white, grey and coral of legs, wings, body and bill. The bill of the Sandwich Tern is black and the Arctic is slightly darker on the breast than the Common. These shades of difference grow more perceptible with a closer familiarity. The Little Tern is the most aerial on its angled wing as the Sandwich is more desultory and its strokes more powerful—in the ceremony of courtship a beautiful slow heave. In diving, the Sandwich is a lesser gannet, hurling itself sheer into the water with a plunge that flings the spray ten feet up in the air; the Little Tern stops dead in the air, hovers in its own radiance of flickered wings, twinkles them over its back with fanned and depressed tail, and half closing them in a shiver of the body casts itself right under, as the Common Tern rarely or never does, rising again with whitebait in a moment, like Anadyomene's charger from its submarine stable.

When the human intruder treads warily (if he be not dead to humanity) among the nests of a large tern colony, the birds form a living canopy of shimmering, transparent web above his head, wheeling through each other's ranks under the heavens, a flying carpet of broken lights taken wing and shaking out a cloud of shrill voices like the grating of the shingle in the sea's teeth. The ear tunes itself to the clamour, and the hoarse screech of the Roseate Tern, the harshest of them all to set against its unearthly beauty, the softer *kirr-rit* of the luminous Sandwich Tern, the bright *chit-chit* of the Little Tern, a note like pebbles gleaming wet, and the steely guttural of the Arctic, beating and swooping frantically a yard above my head, alone among them all for boldness, disentangle themselves like threads of different coloured silk from the fabric of woven sound. He, the Arctic, may well scream like the gales of his home for, with the Roseate, he has one nest of three eggs among the thousand round him, the only record, I believe, of the bird breeding so far south—three gems for the prowling collector.

The eggs and nests of the Common Tern mirror the intense creativeness of this wilderness, an urge of being flooding it like the sea, even more than the mature birds, flung to the air, embody its restlessness of spirit. The eggs of the Roseate Tern are elongated and beautifully zoned with smoky blurs; those of the Little Tern (with a hundred or so nests), similar in brown and grey sprinklings on a light ground to the pear-shaped egg of the ringed plover, do follow within their variations a certain coherence and orderliness of pattern; while of the eighteen nests of the Sandwich Tern, fourteen were unlined, and the large, exquisitely speckled or blotched eggs on a buff, creamy or stone-coloured ground were all laid under the lee of a sand-mound. But with the eggs and nests of the Common Tern, any semblance of uniformity, system, method or symmetry went to the winds, whose caresses into the sand's soft cheek seemed to have dimpled so many of their nests. Caprice in variation was alone

THE VENICE OF ENGLAND

supreme and extended not only to the shape, colour, size and number of the eggs (two were midgets, several were four to a nest, the majority three, and the rest two), but to the position, structure and materials of the nests. They were made indiscriminately in the marram grass, on the sand of the dunes, upon dried mud, in the shingle, at the drift line, among the campion, on the turf, in the herbage, under the nodding fronds of the *Sucæda* bushes, whose shadows enriched the markings of their eggs with wandering pencils. Some were conspicuous at thirty yards, others but natural hollows in the anatomy of the ground. Some were elaborately woven of dried herbs, sticks, seaweed decorated with shells, one was embroidered with an empty capsule of beech mast and a skate's egg-case, while stones were often placed among the eggs. A nest containing light green eggs faintly spotted was a cup of black seaweed, and on the same mound of sand a mere scrape would be cheek by jowl with a piece of architecture. Some were lacquered with broken shells in a shingle depression, and one built of small pebbles hollowed out between three cushions of sea-rocket to its equidistant head and sides. Often the nests bore no sort of relation to the character or materials of the ground whereon they were constructed, being unlined among vegetation and lined away from it, neat or tousled, shallow or deep, as pleased the individual fancy of the bridal pair who made them.

As with the nests, so the eggs, nor was there a

hint of correlation between the two nor between them and the ground they occupied. In ground-colour they varied from green to olive, from grey to all shades of brown from buff to Vandyke, while the markings were as light as mauve or dark as chocolate. Some forms were buff with large stains of brownish-black; others blue-green dotted with Payne's grey. Some were heavily zoned, others dustily, others smokily, others again with a faintly stippled wash. Variations, whether of size, shape or colour, were by no means confined to clutches. One nest contained four eggs, each different both in ground-colour and pattern of spots, and another, dexterously compact, three eggs, one almost oval, the others pear-shaped, with one double the size of its neighbour and all individual in colouring. The print of some blotches, streaks and speckles seemed stamped into the texture of the shell; others seemed broken shadows caught in passing. Exuberance joined with variety to make a spendthrift's holiday.

There is a theory that the variations in the brilliant eggs of the Sandwich Tern are the effect of both sexes incubating them, and so rarely leaving them uncovered to enemies. What then of the prodigality in device of the Common Tern's eggs? The answer is because the freakishness, the whimsies, the fantasies almost of taste in nest construction, all the gay adventures from the adaptive and protective norm of coloration, are not weeded out in the struggle for existence, and they are not so weeded because there is no need to clap upon these tiny hamlets Nature's cap of darkness. It is the terns themselves who are their own defence, not earth's greens, greys and browns. We picked up a wounded tern on the shore away from the ternery and carried this waif and parcel of stricken element light as air, into which had been breathed so wild and rapturous a life, to its fellows—knowing that they would feed it. A party of Greater Black-backed Gulls drifted on ponderous wings as big as clouds among the Ariels of Nature's extra-human thought, and with a scream of rage they set upon them and buffeted them out of the nesting ground. The watcher found a rat on it with its skull perforated by their long sharp bills. It is by the fellowship of mutual aid and concerted action that the terns guard their own, and thus let the djinn out of the bottle. The safety valve of natural selection is removed and the creative force of Nature's life flowers into its full wealth of varied blossom. Some say that these diversities of nest and egg serve the secondary utility of recognition marks, but fundamentally they are the product of each bird's choice, initiative, talent and personality roaming where they will and safe from the shears of the examining Fates.

As we passed, the birds fluttered straight down upon their nests, brooding with their breasts well forward and their tapering wings crossed at a high angle. But as they screamed and circled overhead, moving the heart like a trumpet; as they settled down behind us, making a huge overarching billow of white foam, there fell a sudden hush and spell upon them. In a silence deep as night the whole body massed and in a long column went out like a streamer of white smoke over the dark blue sea. It was as though in that strange movement the curtain raised upon the play and music of elemental powers, of being, of becoming and of dying, went down and left nothing but the uniform expanses of sky and plain.

. . . . . .

The correlations of animate with inanimate nature are so intricate that the least oscillation of the latter from the normal will often make a wilderness of a city or a city of a wilderness. Early in 1922, the sea scored a march against its human foeman on these tidal flats and shingle beaches of Blakeney, and in an impetuous expense of its artillery hammered through a furlong of concrete wall. On one side of the turf bank running between road and beach the land became a shallow broad scrawled over with multiform islands like the hieroglyphs on the yellow-hammer's egg, and on the other water and vegetation came to a deadlock and camped their indiscriminate forces over the ground. Into this tangle of alleys, squares and streets, where the sedges, reeds and water plants made the houses, and the water the open spaces, poured a multitude of birds and founded a city-state in Grecian fashion, but that it was quilted of many nations. Long, crescentic lines of Black-headed Gulls, burnished by

THE VENICE OF ENGLAND

the sun, girdled the seaward frontier of the city, like crusaders after the taking of Jerusalem, and when they rose and drifted out to sea in silver clouds, the city's glittering battlements seemed to have crumbled like Atlantis's that were. A cluster of immature Greater Black-backed Gulls, the van of the hosts which migrate along the coast in the autumn as very symbols of the darkening days, broke in from the north, and in at another gate a troop of sanderling dived in a cascade of white breasts, followed by a single knot who twisted down in the angles of lightning. A throng of cosmopolite citizens ambled the streets and squares in their several national costumes—black and grey coots in their white shields, like the heraldic device of some order, a gallant one judging by the number of duels; green-capped and rufous-belted sheld-duck in white cloaks slashed with black; stockish and massive-billed shovellers in green, white, chestnut and blue with yellow spectacles like aldermen in a free-coloured Morris state; a full-plumaged scaup drake and his white-faced mate (the rarest hyperborean visitors in June), like pochard, with black torso for red, or tufted duck at a distance without the crest; mincing waterhens; lapwings, tourists to Venice from inland plains; herons, lank, primitive and spectral like shadows of their ancestors; swans like the figureheads and hovering terns, the guardian angels of the city; linnets airy as their notes; bustling and hallooing redshank; a tall greenshank like a redshank grown up and lost its mercurial spirits;

dunlin with the black breast-band of the nuptial season; Little Stint like its pigmy form (the urchins of the sandpiper community), and canty Ringed Plover. And as initial verses to this anthology, sounded the skirl of the sedge-warbler, the wheeze of the reed-bunting and the sweeter reed-music of the reed-warbler all along the rushes fringing the turf-bank.

The only unity governing this diversity was one of place, but the nurseries on the other side of the bank had an internal cohesion of common purpose. Two small islands almost flat with the water and shagged with tussocks of marram, other wiry grasses and coarse turf and patched with dry mud, held about eight hundred nests of Sandwich and Common Terns, black-headed gulls, ringed plover and redshank. They were mingled helter-skelter, lined or unlined, slovenly or compact, many so close together as to be semi-detached (the nine Sandwich Terns' nests were within an orbit of three yards), and with eggs so variously shaded and mottled as to make classification of size rather than pattern, colouration or even shape the clue to identity of species. The terns' eggs and nests ran riot in idiosyncrasy, but those of the gulls were hardly less variable—spotted, zoned and splashed with greys, blacks and browns of every tone, on a ground of olive, green, buff, dark brown or blue. Gulls are of a plover-like ancestry, and the Black-head, diverging first to a sea-habit, then a land-habit, and here breeding almost within the spray of high tide, was with his

THE VENICE OF ENGLAND

fancy-roaming eggs and nests consistent in plasticity. One of them was a monument, a palace, a foot high, built on the highest point of the island and broad based on a straddling foundation of interlacing sticks thinning to the grassy apex of the pyramid, on which reposed, like a single blossom topping a bush or one lasting poem out of a lifetime of verses, a solitary egg. This pair alone among their brethren, some with mere twists of grass, had the synoptic view of life; they saw it whole in one sweep from the experience of memory to the prevision of inference; what tides have done before, spoke the tight logic of stick upon stick, tides may do again. Only the lovely treasure of the redshank, with its background of yellow or grey or both (lighter than the lapwing's) and its rich daubs of purples and browns, is concealed in the heart of a tussock, where long grasses play their shadows over it, the fingers of the wind's caress.

Past the sheld-duck on the water, gowned so comely and so bizarre both with her ducklings in their white down banded twice with Vandyke lines, and over on the mainland, the shelf between inland and outer sea, was an oyster-catcher's nest with the rare number of four eggs (streaked and printed grey-brown on a yellowish-grey ground-colour) walled with pebbles in a shingle depression, and one was double-yolked and twice the size of the others, an oddity to make itch the thievish hand of the collector. Once an egg of this same pair rolled out of its hollow nearer the water, and they swung round and round the watcher's head, wailfully *kleep-kleeping*, until he went to the nest and restored the egg. As I walked over the island the gulls hung screaming low over my head, a roof woven of white wings with the azure one of the world streaming through it. Here were three skies and I marooned on a cloud in the lowest, but only the middle one lived with me and that was all life, broken not only into a mosaic of moving lights but into full a thousand entities of brain and heart and nerve, and among them how many originals like that pair of gulls and oyster-catchers? The city was on one side of the bank, its corporate life on the other, for eggs and nests were safe in fancy-freedom by a common purpose of watch and ward which kept the peace within the ranks of the divers peoples (the gulls, as I was assured and could see for myself, did not touch the terns', redshanks' or plovers' eggs) and every enemy except man and the elements without.

If there is no more individual shore-bird than the redshank, there is none so personable as the Ringed Plover. In social flight when the flock becomes an individual and the birds its several organic parts like the words of a lyric, they resemble sanderling, Little Stint and dunlin; they nest among the terns and gulls, as their fellow-waders (except the redshank) never do, and their charming little pear-shaped eggs, three and sometimes four, are similar, but for shape and position with their narrower ends together in the middle of the nest, to the Little

THE VENICE OF ENGLAND

Tern's. They are not quite so variable in markings, but I found one nest of four eggs with one pair pigmented to type and the other, cream-coloured, without markings of any kind. The sides of the cupped nest are usually embossed with pebbles and broken shells, but I have seen a few nests among the gulls wound with grass bents. The birds are true to the volatile expression of their homes, impinged upon by the restless sea, suffused and rarefied by the elements, and they twinkle over their native shore with a run which seems another phase of flight, but always more waywardly than other small shore-birds, while their plumper and squatter build gives them an inexplicable pathos. Thus they maintain a fellowship of habit with their various associates and yet preserve an essence, unique and particular, of their own.

There is an infallible method of finding out whether ringed plover have eggs or young. If the former, they content themselves with flying in circles round the intruder, with their soft plaints —*peep, peep*, and *toolee, toolee*, the dissyllable being the nuptial call modulated into a quavering trill, when the male weaves his flight-mazes or slides along the ground with humped back and dragging wing. But if the latter, then the female becomes a Lyceum tragic actress in the convulsions of death. Actually she mimics the throes, creeping along in painful spasms with one wing flapping in the air, the other lolling as though broken, and then with head half buried in the shingle, rolls over from side to side, and with a last shudder agonises into a lifeless, tumbled heap. I am a stoat; my craving for blood is whetted and I bare my teeth as I pad after her. A last paroxysm of life spurts up in her and carries her writhing and floundering another twenty yards. A bestial possession foams the blood through my arteries and I go bounding after her, my snout dilated at the anticipated scent of her blood—and there she is flashing her silver wings over my head with a "hey-nonny-toolee, and keep you low, my child, till I entice him this way and that way far out of yours." The crouching infant three or four hours old, in down of fawn and grey, rucks its nape feathers over the telling black collar and shams stone, but stones do not pulsate, nor when picked up wave stumps of wings and set off on long shanks to tumble head over ears over a rather bigger member of their order. The nest a few yards off has still one egg but no broken shells, which are carried off the nesting ground to give the younglings, one supposes, room and warmth under the parent's breast at night.

The little "dotterels," as they are called locally, are, further, much more circumspect in going on to their eggs than the terns, who come home down the chimney, so to speak. The female returns in a series of runs and pauses, retreats, approaches, goes off at a tangent, sidles nearer, swerves away again, and finally makes a dash for it and settles deeply in with a sigh rippling all over her body.

The eye leaves her, jumps over the waving beds

THE VENICE OF ENGLAND

of sea-campion, threads its way among the hulks of the seals basking on the sand-spit and launches out to sea, crossing the pale bar of the horizon into the immensity of space. The loneliness of the human mind is behind it and it travels further than any winged citizen of this busy township, contented in the fulfilment of its single and commingled lives. And in space that mind is at home, building it with cities of its own workmanship, where all our quest is ended, our frustrations undone, and as these birds know a matchless freedom of body here, so we there an equal freedom of the mind.

WILLIAM MORRIS

By Alfred Noyes

WILLIAM MORRIS, " poet, artist, manufacturer, and socialist," was born on 24th March, 1834. He went up to Exeter College, Oxford, in January 1853, with a considerable knowledge and love of architecture, poetry, and old stories. He went up at a time when "all reading men were Tennysonians; and all sets of reading men talked poetry"; when, moreover, the spirit of Darwin was brooding over the intellectual world and the Crimean war was about to set the younger generation thinking about schemes of social regeneration. All creeds and systems were going into the intellectual melting-pot. Nothing was a very sure refuge for the mind but the beauty of the visible world as revealed and made enduring in art. Everything else appeared to be changing, decaying, passing away. The visible world itself was not so beautiful as it had once been. Art was the consoler of the pessimists and the redeemer of the optimists. Ruskin was the prophet of the new religion, " the religion of beauty "; and hundreds that had grown sick of the controversial wrangles of the time were turning to

WILLIAM MORRIS

it for relief with all the passion which their forefathers would have felt in seeking the consolations of the Church. Morris himself, when he came up to Oxford, has been described as a High Churchman and a Neo-Catholic. It may very confidently be affirmed that he was neither more nor less than a worshipper of beauty, and that the ritual of the Church was nothing more or less to him than a form of style.

> 'Twas in Church on Palm Sunday
> Listening what the priest did say
> Of the kiss that did betray,
>
> That the thought did come to me
> How the olives used to be
> Growing in Gethsemane.
>
> That the thoughts upon me came
> Of the lantern's steady flame,
> Of the softly whispered name.
>
> Of how kiss and words did sound
> While the olives stood around,
> While the robe lay on the ground.
>
> Then the words the Lord did speak
> And that kiss in Holy Week
> Dreams of many a kiss did make:
>
> Lovers kiss beneath the moon,
> With it sorrow cometh soon:
> Juliet's within the tomb:
>
> Angelico's in quiet light,
> 'Mid the aureoles very bright
> God is looking from the height.
>
> There the monk his love doth meet;—

and so forth, he wrote, in a poem which he sent to Cormell Price (not included in any of his volumes). And it is obvious that he was not exactly listening to "what the priest did say" from a "High Churchman's" point of view, but simply and solely from the point of view of an artist. Even in church he was striving to build a "shadowy isle of bliss mid-most the beatings of the steely sea." He was probably aided and abetted in this by the great friendship of his Oxford days which is, prehaps, the most important fact of that period of his life—the friendship he formed with Burne-Jones, who had also gone up to Exeter College in 1853.

He was "aided and abetted," I say, because I do not think he was influenced very much by Burne-Jones or by any one else. His life has a very extraordinary completeness and coherence. It is a happy chance that the whole childhood of William Morris may be seen at a glance, as on a single splendid fragment of his own romance-empurpled tapestry. About the year 1841, any one wandering near Woodford Hall, on the borders of Epping Forest, and within sight of the clear Thames, with its "white and ruddy-brown sails moving among cornfields," might have been surprised by the vision of a curly-haired young knight in glittering armour, riding through the strange glades of hornbeam on one of Titania's palfreys, a pony such as in fairyland might have been "tethered to a poppy or stabled in a tree." But here, in broad noon, it was pacing proudly beneath a greaved and breastplated young warrior from Joyous Gard, a child-champion shining through the fairy-fringes of that sunny nook of unspoilt England, like some virgin star through the branches of Broceliande, in quest of the "beauty folded up in forests old!" The small knight-errant was, of course, no ghost of Galahad or Percivale, but the future poet of the *Earthly Paradise*; and his age was about seven summers.

The prosaic interpretation of this picture is that he had been given a toy suit of armour; but as he made such use of it we may safely assume that it corresponded to a desire of his own; and, indeed, it seems in a sense the natural outcome, the glittering crystallisation as it were, of all the other external facts and features of his childhood's kingdom—that wonderful Wood beyond our world's end, which can only be entered upon the wings of poetry, but can never even be approached along the crawling highways of reason. The picture is worthy of note, because it really does help to establish at the outset the spiritual continuity of Morris's life, and to show, for instance, that Mr. Swinburne was justified in saying of Morris's first volume, *The Defence of Guenevere*: "It seems to have been now lauded and now decried as the result and expression of a school rather than a man, of a theory or tradition than a poet . . . those who so judged were blind guides. Such things as were in this book are taught and learnt in no school but that of instinct. Upon no piece of work in the world was the impress of native character ever more distinctly stamped, more deeply branded."

It may not be inappropriate here to say a word about the technique of that first book. On a question of this kind it is only with great diffidence that one would care to dissent from Mr. Swinburne, who finds it to be blundering and stumbling, and altogether very faulty, and regards Morris very much as an amateur in the matter of the craft of versification. The merit of the book—according to Mr. Swinburne—lies almost entirely in its passion, emotional depth, and truth. But this is probably due to the fact that Morris aimed at something very different from the aims of Mr. Swinburne. He never attempted to write lines "of their own arduous fullness reverent." He often deliberately ignored the aids to that fullness which are given by elision; and elision — Mr. Swinburne says — is a law, not a privilege. But Morris aimed at an effect which he chould only obtain by his own methods. His verses should be read slowly, almost syllable by syllable, with due regard to their child-like *naïveté*, and the reader will soon perceive that a poem like *The Defence of Guenevere*, with its extraordinarily overlapping lines, and rhymes so unexpected that at first sight they seem rambling and bungling, is a consummate work of art. The feverish wanderings of the half-distraught queen's speech could not have been rendered more magnificently than in this curiously-wrought piece of *terza-rima*. On the subject of Morris's verse we are compelled to differ from Mr. Swinburne, though we cannot enter into the matter very fully here.

Never was Art more the child of Memory than in the case of William Morris. His early days at Woodford Hall were, consciously or unconsciously, a fount of inspiration to the end of his life. The self-contained mediæval system of the house and the old festivals that it observed must have meant a good deal to the imaginative youngster who made it his playground. Twelfth Night was one of the great days of the year at Woodford Hall, and the masque of St. George was always then presented with considerable elaboration. It is probably not too fanciful to say that this determined the character of some of the masque-like poems in Morris's first volume and, perhaps, even of the later morality play, *Love is Enough*. Those who know childhood best will be the most likely to go further and say that some of the peculiarly vivid hunting, roasting, and feasting passages in *Jason* derive some of their glamour from that early proximity of Epping Forest, and the fact that as a child William Morris was allowed to roast the rabbits and fieldfares which he shot for his own supper. It was an affair of the imagination even in those earliest days; for we are told that his great ambition was to shoot his game with bow and arrows. Like most great men, Morris retained his childhood to an exceptional degree; and, with all due deference to the critics, who find a more solemn import in the mere fact that he endeavours " to take up the lost threads of the mediæval artistic tradition," I can only see him still "making believe," attempting to build his shadowy isle of bliss, yearning to shoot his game with bow and arrows, and striving to recapture the happiness of his own childhood's kingdom.

Morris's father had a great liking for the old churches in the neighbourhood of Woodford Hall, with their monuments and brasses; and his young son used to accompany him on visits to them. When he was eight years old William Morris was taken to see Canterbury. On the same holiday he saw the church of Minster in Thanet, and it is said that fifty years later, never having seen it in the interval, he described the church in some detail from that memory. "Gothic architecture" could have been little more than a romantic phrase to him at that age; yet if his father really loved it and spoke simply to him about it, a spire might seem more like a soaring prayer to a child than anything built with hands could seem to a man. At any rate the glorious impression that the individual scenes left upon him is indubitable. It must be remembered that they meant—at the very least —great pillars and dark aisles and stained glass and dim rich streaming lights over cold mysterious tombs. It must be remembered that they meant curious inscriptions and strange recumbent figures in eternal armour, with frozen swords and stark upturned feet. The memory certainly survives in the *Guenevere* volume, and gives it much of its atmosphere. The *naïveté* of some of its language

WILLIAM MORRIS

is that of a child rather than of the Middle Ages. For instance, when Rapunzel sings—

> My mother taught me prayers
> To say when I had need;
> I have so many cares,
> That I can take no heed
> Of many words in them;
> But I remember this:

was ever the very spirit of childhood voiced so perfectly as in the lines that follow—though the child itself be only seen through a stained-glass window darkly?—

> Yet besides *I have made this
> By myself*: Give me a kiss,
> Dear God, dwelling up in heaven!
>
> . . . . .
>
> Yea, besides, I have made this:
> Lord, give Mary a dear kiss,
> And let gold Michael, who look'd down,
> When I was here, on Rouen town
> From the spire, bring me that kiss
> On a lily! Lord do this!

It is curious, too, how the dumb stone of *King Arthur's Tomb* seems to make almost a third character in that wonderful interview between Guenevere and Lancelot. The tomb itself is hardly mentioned, but the reader gradually gets an almost physical realisation of its palpable and stony presence; and, though it was in later years that Morris acquired his knowledge, one may quite safely affirm it to have been his childhood that gave the glamour when he wrote—

> Edward the king is dead, at Westminster
> The carvers smooth the curls of his long beard.

ALFRED NOYES

This atmosphere pervades the whole of Morris's first volume, and though it may be said to belong to the manner of his school, it belongs also to an architectural region which the other Pre-Raphaelite poets left comparatively unexplored, a region into which it may quite justly be said that Morris first wandered in his own childhood and apart from any influence but that of his own father.

In the childhood of most impressionable people there are usually one or two moments, events, or landmarks of which the memory is as vivid throughout the whole of their lives as the foot-prints on the sand in *Robinson Crusoe*. It is probable, for instance, that Stevenson in his childhood had been tremendously impressed, and perhaps terrified, by some blind beggar with a tapping stick like those that appear in *Treasure Island* and *Kidnapped*. However that may be, there are two early imprints upon the mind of William Morris that probably —taken with the rest of his early environment— would count for quite as much in determining his choice of the Middle Ages for his "form of style" as any later influence. One of these is the fact that when he lived at Woodford Hall there were stocks and a cage there on a bit of wayside green in the middle of the village; and he himself has said in a letter to his daughter, that he used to regard them with considerable terror and decidedly preferred to walk on the other side of the road. To my mind there is not the slightest doubt that this early and imaginative dread is responsible for the extraordinarily vivid sense of terror with regard to such instruments which he displays in depicting Sir Peter Harpdon's torture. The second of these foot-prints on the sand he has recorded in his *Lecture on the Lesser Arts of Life*: "Well I remember as a boy my first acquaintance with a room hung with faded greenery at Queen Elizabeth's Lodge, by Chingford Hatch, in Epping Forest, and the impression of romance that it made upon me! a feeling that always comes back on me when I read Sir Walter Scott's *Antiquary* and come to the description of the Green Room at Monkbarns, amongst which the novelist has imbedded the fresh and glittering verses of the summer poet Chaucer: yes, that was more than upholstery, believe me."

It is quite possible that here we have Morris's first little private gateway into the greenwoods of Chaucer. At any rate, it is quite obvious that all his adventures were really his own, and that he made his own discoveries of beauty as he went along his own winding path. As a rule it is not profitable to indulge in such conjectures and suggestions as the foregoing; but the case of Morris is exceptional; and as he has been so often treated in the Pre-Raphaelite manner as one of a school, it becomes all the more desirable to show the unity and continuity of his intellectual life. Not only were his sense-perceptions extremely acute, but his memory of them and all their associations was extraordinary. It was not only big things like churches that he was able to remember for fifty years after seeing them once in childhood. "To this day," wrote Morris in his latter years, "the smell of May reminds me of going to bed by daylight." Those who fully understand what such a remark implies will also understand what we mean by saying that Woodford Hall, his early home, was the germ of all Morris's later work. He extended the boundaries of his world; but he never shifted its centre. Woodford Hall, with the clear Thames flowing past its door, and the scents of the Maytide in its garden, and the bloom of the plums upon its walls, was at the heart of all his works, even when he became a Socialist. It thrust itself up through his theories like the boughs of the Branstock through the hall of the Niblungs. More perhaps than any other English poet, Morris gives expression to that emotion which Tennyson called "the passion of the past." In Morris this passion is intense to the point of pain. It appears under many disguises. His Utopias of the past, though he projected them into the future, were in many of their aspects hardly more than a lyrical cry for his own dead days. His tales of the Middle Ages are as it were remembered from a past of nearer date, a past in which he had himself lived. Woodford Hall was the nucleus of that "shadowy isle of bliss" which William Morris was ever afterwards striving to build—for himself and for others—midmost the beatings of the world's bitter and steely sea. At Kelmscott Manor, which he loved so dearly that he broke down when forced to leave it; or on a tub at Hammersmith, that was his only strife—to realise the Earthly Paradise. The Earthly Paradise was enough for him. He, indeed, desired no golden groves or quiet seats of the just. The sights and sounds and scents of the immediate Maytime were all that he desired. But these, with the youth that seemed necessary to complete them, were ever passing away. *Passing Away* is the burden of his poetry—so much so that one might almost say it is possessed with the long anguish of the fear of death. The only philosophical utterance he ever made about the matter was that perhaps change and death were necessary or there would be no good stories—our finest stories being those that told of oldest and saddest happenings. And when he was brought face to face with the fact that he could not "make quick-coming death a little thing, or bring again the pleasure of past years," he turned instinctively to the Middle Ages as a permanent and definite form of style, beyond the reach of change, whereby he might embody what he loved and raise it above the beatings of that bitter sea. He turned to the Middle Ages not as a mere æsthete seeking an anodyne, but as a child turns to fairyland. It was his method of removing what he loved out of space and time in order to view it in the light of eternity. He deliberately adopted the convention that made Troy a belfried town like Bruges and Chartres, because he felt that this, too, was another method of defying time, and that he had thus in some strange way the power of building himself a continuing city. He felt an altogether modern and scholarly pleasure in the anachronism, a little shock of delight as he brought the facts of history into collision and resolved the resultant discord into harmony by a deeper note. He felt a peculiarly modern pleasure as his fabled cities rose to music, a pleasure that separates him by many centuries from Chaucer (to whom he is often very carelessly likened) on the one hand; while there is a depth of sincere feeling, a passionate desire, a reality of self-expression, living and breathing through it all which entirely differentiates his work from that of the perverse and paradoxical æsthetes who followed him. His world is an entirely remembered one; and it is largely this that gives his work vitality, and sets it apart from the work of Wardour Street connoisseurs. It is Morris's craving to capture the golden moments that slipped out of his own living hands (a craving of the same kind as that expressed by Keats in his Odes) which lifts his work, not so much in great single lines as in its whole wistful atmosphere, to the level of high poetry. It is this that fills it with the light of that Eternity which he always refrained from attempting to fathom; and it is this that allows one to see in his pictures of earthly beauty that high intellectual passion which, conscious or unconscious, is the first essential to great art. First and last, art is religion. There is no room in it for preciosity—no room in it for anything but the Eternal. There was no preciosity in William Morris's choice of the Middle

Ages as his " form of style." He turned to them quite naturally, as world-weary men turn to their childhood, knowing perhaps that except as a little child in glittering armour he could not enter into his Kingdom of Heaven.

WILLIAM JAMES AND HIS WORK
By Charles M. Bakewell

"He was so commanding a presence, so curious and inquiring, so responsive and expansive, and so generous and reckless of himself and of his own, that every one said of him: 'Here is no musty *savant*, but a man, a great man, a man on the heroic scale, not to serve whom is avarice and sin.'" So James speaks with affection of his own teacher Agassiz, and the words fitly describe the impression he himself made upon his students and associates. There was none who did not come under the spell of his personality, none who did not look forward eagerly to every fresh work from his pen. There was such a sense of life and reality in all that he wrote that reading his works had, in a peculiar sense, the charm of personal intercourse. It was like meeting the man himself and sharing in his faith, his enthusiasm, his vision.

One does not think of James as a man with a philosophy, but rather as one who cleared the decks for all future philosophising. Late in life, to be sure, he labelled his view "pragmatism," modestly declaring this to be a "new name for some old ways of thinking," and dedicating the book in which the view was presented to John Stuart Mill, from whom he first learned the "pragmatic openness of mind." But he is careful to explain that the word stands for a method, and for a theory of truth, rather than for a system of philosophy. And when the view was launched and began to have followers, instinctively he shrank from the use of the label. When a philosophy, even his own, had been ticketed and had become one among many philosophical *isms*, it began to lose some of its vitality.

At very rare intervals in the history of philosophy there have appeared thinkers who, like William James, are too real to be readily classified—thinkers who cut under the distinctions that divide men into schools. When they appear they always speak the language of the people, for the simple reason that they are interpreting life as real men live it with a freshness of vision unknown in the schools. The influence of William James has probably travelled further and gone deeper than that of any other American scholar. Into the languages of all civilised peoples his works have been translated, and everywhere they have met with instant recognition. Honorary degrees, honorary memberships in learned societies and academies, all manner of scholarly distinctions poured in upon him from all quarters. And yet by far the larger part of his published works consists of essays and addresses first delivered to popular or semi-popular audiences; and even his most technical performance, his classic work in psychology, is singularly simple and direct and free from technicalities, and withal readable. The fact is significant, and explains in part the secret of his hold upon his contemporaries. For, though writing for the people, he was never a populariser. He did not have tucked away in his den some profound and recondite system clothed in the polysyllabic profundity which learning too often affects, which, on occasion, he condescended to translate, in diluted doses, for the benefit of laymen. He could not help being simple and clear, for he lived close to reality in its concrete fullness; and he could not help writing for the people, and not for a special academic guild, because he believed in the people, and because, furthermore, he believed in the mission of philosophy to help the people to interpret life and to lay hold of life's ideals, and thus to " know a good man when they saw him."

James tells us that it was the hours he spent with Agassiz that "so taught him the difference between all possible abstractionists and all livers in the light of the world's concrete fullness" that he was never able to forget it. And the term which, by preference, he used to describe his position was "radical empiricism," a phrase which shows the importance he ascribed to method in philosophising. How far removed this method is from that which commonly passes for empiricism one can best find out by reading the last chapter in his larger *Psychology*. Without going into details, it is enough here to note that for him the method meant simply a recognition of the fact that " the truth of things is after all their living fullness." To lay hold of the facts in their living fullness was what he meant by being radically empirical. But the facts of human nature are so intimate and so familiar that they usually escape observation. Or if they chance to be called to our attention, they are apt to be summarily lumped together under some familiar caption, or forthwith named and classified in a conventional way, and thus disposed of. James could always "see the familiar as if it were strange," and was thus peculiarly fitted for the rôle of explorer and observer of the familiar, but little known, facts of the inner life. Moreover, he appreciated as few have done the extent to which words and phrases, dogmas and ready-made principles of classification, blind men's vision and dull their senses. To the facts of experience with which psychology and ethics deal he brought the artist's skill in pure appreciation of values, and he possessed a rare gift for describing what he saw. His special contributions to psychology, and his significance in philosophy, are alike due to this trait.

The first lesson of radical empiricism is that the mind never is merely a passive spectator, never is merely a receptacle for data supplied from without. Such a way of viewing experience is to mistake for the mind what a real mind never is, and for data what real data never are. In a striking passage James writes:

The world's contents are *given* to each of us in an order so foreign to our subjective interests that we can hardly by an effort of the imagination picture to ourselves what it is like. We have to break that order altogether—and by picking out from it the items which concern us, and connecting them with others far away, which we say " belong " with them, we are able to make out definite threads of sequence and tendency; to foresee particular liabilities and get ready for them; and to enjoy simplicity and harmony in place of what was chaos. . . . Can we realise for an instant what a cross-section of all existence at a definite point of time would be? While I talk and the flies buzz, a sea-gull catches a fish at the mouth of the Amazon, a tree falls in the Adirondack wilderness, a man sneezes in Germany, a horse dies in Tartary, and twins are born in France. What does that mean? Does the contemporaneity of these events with one another and with a million others as disjointed form a rational bond between them, and unite them into anything that means for us a world? Yet just such a collateral contemporaneity, and nothing else, is the real order of the world. It is an order with which we have nothing to do but to get away from it as fast as possible. As I said, we break it; we break it into histories, and we break it into arts, and we break it into sciences; and then we begin to feel at home. We make ten thousand separate serial orders of it, and on any one of these we react as though the others did not exist.[1]

Other philosophies had indeed noted this truth before. But hitherto philosophy has been too much influenced by the model of mathematics and physics, and has thus tended to think in terms of the contrast between form and matter. To-day biological sciences are in the ascendant, and they furnish a safer model for philosophy inasmuch as they bring

[1] " Reflex Action and Theism," *The Will to Believe*, pp. 118, 119.

WILLIAM JAMES AND HIS WORK

us nearer to the facts in their concrete fullness. The contrast is between the living and the dead; and life means growth, development, progress, and time is of the essence of experience. The complexity of experience upon which James laid stress was that which it receives in its time dimension. The time quality of experience is its most significant trait. Everywhere we find fluency and continuity, and in all our interpretations, scientific as well as philosophical, the practical categories are dominant. Our philosophy is essentially forward-looking, and must measure values in results, truth values as well as moral values. Hence James was not interested in truth in the abstract, but rather in the actual process of truth-getting—in what happens when an idea is accepted as true; and he noted that ideas passed for true in proportion to their serviceableness in guiding us through the tangled complexity of experience, in making us at home in the world in which we daily live, and thus masters of it. Science itself was a human construction for human ends. And when it gave itself airs, became sacrosanct and absolute, as it did in the positivism of Herbert Spencer, and in the name of science proceeded to rule out of court all those facts and values of the spiritual life which do not admit of verification through the senses, it ceased to be science, and became a sheer philosophical dogmatism. It was in fact no better than those pretentious idealisms which in the name of abstract reason made all things parts of one inclusive whole, made the world a "block universe," fixed, eternal, perfect, and left no room for what makes life for the individual significant—freedom, choice, novelty, and progress.

Ideals again were not decorations of life in the abstract, highly polished moral ornaments; they were the practical tools of good living. They were not to be measured by the noble language in which they were expressed, nor yet by the subjective feelings or emotions they aroused, but by the way they worked, by what they actually accomplished in the prosaic world of dust and dirt and brute fact, for the betterment of character and of the conditions of human life. The truth is that our life, intellectual and moral, is at every turn ruled by ideals, and back of all ideals lies faith—a faith involving a certain element of risk from which none can escape. And much of James's work is spent in defending the faiths by which men actually live, by testing them in the only manner in which their truth can be tested, by the way in which they express themselves in life.

James also possessed in a wonderful degree what might be called sympathetic imagination—the ability to get as it were on the inside of the other fellow's vision; and whenever he ran across, in the work of another thinker, however humble and obscure, evidence of some fresh and original interpretation of genuine experience, he heralded it as a veritable discovery. It was a new document to be reckoned with. He was, in fact, singularly free from what

WILLIAM JAMES AND HIS WORK

he has called "a certain blindness in human beings." How free, a reading of the *Varieties of Religious Experience* will show. The essay in which he discusses this blindness is, as he says, more than the piece of sentimentalism that at first sight it might appear to be. "It connects itself with a definite view of the world and of our moral relations to it." That view is the pluralistic or individualistic philosophy according to which "the truth is too great for any one actual mind, even though that mind be dubbed 'the absolute,' to know the whole of it. The facts and worths of life need many cognisers to take them in. There is no point of view absolutely public and universal." The practical consequence of this philosophy is, he adds, the "well-known democratic respect for the sacredness of individuality."

Perhaps the chief reason for the popularity of James's philosophy is the sense of freedom it brings with it. It is the philosophy of open doors; the philosophy of a new world with a large frontier and, beyond, the enticing unexplored lands where one may still expect the unexpected; a philosophy of hope and promise, a philosophy that invites adventure, since it holds that the dice of experience are not loaded. The older monistic philosophies and religions present by contrast stuffy closed systems and an exhausted universe. They seem to pack the individual into a logical strait-jacket and to represent all history as simply the unfolding of a play that was written to its very last line from the dawn of creation. These old absolutisms go with the old order of things.

James is an interpreter of the new order of democracy. The most important and interesting thing about a nation, or an historic epoch, as about an individual, was, he held, its "ideals and over-beliefs." And if he is our representative philosopher of democracy, it is not because of his individualism, his appreciation of the unique, the uncommunicable, his hospitality of mind, his respect for humanity in its every honest manifestation, his support of the doctrine of live and let live, his tolerance of all that was not itself intolerant; it is not because of his insistence that professions be measured by their "cash value" in experience, and men by their ability to "make good"; but it is, above all, because of his skill in interpreting those ideals and over-beliefs of his nation and epoch. For these are the things that save democracy from vulgarity and commercialism, that preserve the higher human qualities, and ensure for the citizens of a free land the fruits of civilisation—more air, more refinement, and a more liberal perspective.

James was a firm believer in democracy. But he held that democracy was still on trial, and that no one could tell how it would stand the ordeal. "Nothing future," he writes, "is quite secure; states enough have inwardly rotted; and democracy as a whole may undergo self-poisoning. But, on the other hand, democracy is a kind of religion, and we are bound not to admit its failure. Faiths and utopias are the noblest exercise of human reason, and no one with a spark of reason in him will sit down fatalistically before the croaker's picture. The best of us are filled with the contrary vision of a democracy stumbling through every error till its institutions glow with justice and its customs shine with beauty. Our better men *shall* show the way and we *shall* follow them. . . . The ceaseless whisper of the more permanent ideals, the steady tug of truth and justice, give them but time, *must* warp the world in their direction." [1]

[1] *Memories and Studies*, pp. 317 ff.

THE FIVE IMAGES OF LOVE

By Grace Rhys

No one understands the nature of love; it is like a bird of heaven that sings a strange language. It lights down among us, coming from whence we know not, going we know not how or when, striking out wild notes of music that make even fatigued and heavy hearts to throb and give back a tone of courage.

The sorts and kinds of love are infinite in number, infinite as the days of the years of time. Each one of us is capable of many and various loves. We cannot love two creatures, not two dogs, with the same love. To each of those whom we love we offer a gem of different colour and value;—to the unknown Master of the heavens, ah! who shall tell of what sort is the love we offer to Him? Yet in this love, too (which is natural worship), we discover the same vibrational atmosphere that invades the soul of all lovers.

I doubt we shall not get much nearer to the nature of love by mere talking. Intellectual statements are of little use. God does not make intellectual statements, He creates. We have to find our way about in the vast medley of created

THE FIVE IMAGES OF LOVE

things that life spreads out around us, and pick up what bits of knowledge we can as we make our way along.

Let me choose five images that will give an idea of what the awaking of this new life means.

I. Shall we not say that the creature without love is like the lamp unlit? There it is, and no one needs it. But touch it with flame, and it trembles and glows and becomes the centre of the room where it stands. Everything that falls under its rays is new-gilt. So does the lover see all natural things quite new.

II. Or take the image of the withering plant that is dying of drought. The sun's rays have parched it; the roots have searched and searched for moisture in a soil that grows every day harder and drier. The plant wilts and hangs its head; it is fainting and ready to die, when down comes the rain in a murmuring multitude of round scented drops, the purest thing alive, a distilled essence, necessary to life. Under that baptism the plant lifts itself up; it drinks and rejoices. In the night it renews its strength; in the morning the heat it has had from the sun, reinforced by the rain, bursts out into coloured flowers. So I have known a man battered by hard life and the excess of his own passions: I have seen love come to such a man and take him up and cleanse him and set him on his feet; and from him has burst forth a flood of colour and splendour—creative work that now lends its fiery stimulus to thousands.

III. Another image might be of the harp that stands by itself in golden aloofness. Then come the beautiful arms, the curving fingers that pluck at the strings, and the air is filled with melody; the harp begins to live, thrilling and rejoicing, down to its golden foot.

IV. Or picture the unlighted house, empty at fall of night. The windows are dark; the door shut; the clean wind goes about and about it, and cannot find an entrance. The dull heavy air is faint within; it longs to be reunited to the wind of the world outside. Then comes the woman with the key, and in she steps; the windows are opened, the imprisoned air rushes out, the wind enters; the lamps and the fire are lit; so that light fills windows and doors. The tables are set, there is the sound of footsteps; and more footsteps. The house glows and lives.

One could please oneself by many more images; such as the white garment of feathers that the young swans put on in the spring: the young flowers opening out their cups to the Sun that fills them with his golden wine. All life is full of such images, because nature has ruled that love, energy, beauty, and joy are one.

V. A last image only I would like to add because of the pleasure it has given me. On the north door of the Cathedral of Chartres there is a sculptured design, some six hundred years old, of God creating the birds. God is charming, quite young, not more than thirty-eight or so; He has a most sweet expression. Behind Him a little

THE FIVE IMAGES OF LOVE

stands the Son, about seventeen, tall as He and very like Him, but beardless. He has the same sweetness of look, as though upon each countenance an ineffable smile were just dawning. The Father is holding something that time has broken in His hand; most likely it is a bird. What a fortunate moment! What a fortunate thought! No wonder they both look pleased. Never have the birds disappointed Him as have we, His ruder children. Every spring since then these small creatures praise Him, head turned skywards, for the joy of the beloved, for the secret nest.

Imagining and pondering, one is apt to grow a little wise; now perhaps we may say that love is a radiant atmosphere of the soul, a celestial energy, a fluid force.

This force, this energy is set running in the wide kingdom that is within us by some Spirit touch. A soft tumult takes place in the life within; waves on waves of joy, desire, grief, ecstasy begin to run, making a trembling music that often causes the whole body to shake and tremble too.

I am in love with love; I do adore it;—from the smile on that rough fellow's face as he talks to his dog, to the ardours of a St. Francis or a Joan of Arc. That bright creative flame, winged, conferring the gift of tongues, master of all music, of all joy, is the best thing we have of life.

THE RECREATIONS OF THE SPITAL-FIELDS WEAVERS

By Edmond G. A. Holmes

I AM told that somewhere on this planet of ours there is a fastidious professor who holds that the lower orders (as we call them) ought to be kept in a state of semi-serfdom, in order that the upper classes may have leisure for culture. If this paradoxical theory were put forward as a paradox there might be something to be said for it; at any rate one might treat it as a joke and pass it by with a smile; but I understand that it is put forward in all seriousness; and, this being so, I propose to subject it to serious criticism; and I do so the more readily because in our fastidious professor I recognise one of my own dead selves.

The first and most obvious objection to this thesis is that the enslavement, or semi-enslavement, of the lower orders is too high a price to pay for any end, however intrinsically desirable.

A second and almost equally obvious objection is that if culture demands for its advancement the permanent degradation of seven-eighths of the human race, in the very act of making this claim it proves that its estimate of its own worth is unduly high. For if the effect of culture on the cultured is to make them so callously selfish that they will accept with complacence the sacrifice to their supposed interests of the well-being of the masses —their comfort, their leisure and their economic freedom—it is most emphatically *not* the humanising influence which it pretends to be.

A third objection to the theory is that it stultifies its own *raison d'être*. For what is the meaning, what is the value of culture? Is it a precious possession, the mere existence of which exalts and enriches the human race? Surely not. Surely it must be used and enjoyed, surely we must feed upon it in our hearts, if its potential value is to be converted into actual value. But if seven-eighths of the human race are to be forbidden to enjoy it, if they are to be denied the education and the leisure which might enable them to enjoy it, of what value will it be when produced? Of what value is culture if it is to be reserved exclusively for the delectation of a clique of connoisseurs and dilettantists, with a band of scholars and a few men of creative genius scattered among these, and is not to enlighten and elevate the mass of mankind?

A fourth objection, the most serious of all from our professor's point of view, is that the theory defeats its own avowed aim; that, if carried out, it would make for the degradation, not for the advancement of culture. For culture, like a mountain, should be broad-based if it is to rise to a lofty height; but, according to the theory which I am examining, it is of the essence of culture that it should have a narrow base, that it should be an Eiffel Tower or a sky-scraper, not a Mont Blanc. The great mountain, as Ruskin has well said, lifts the lowlands on to its sides. It is only by lifting the lowlands, by using them as the lower courses of its own structure, that it has been able to rise so high above them. The Eiffel Tower spurned the lowlands. It tried to take a short cut to heaven. But because it had made no attempt to identify itself with the lowlands or to incorporate them in its own structure, it failed ignominiously and had to be cut off, lest it should topple over, when it had reached the level of one of the humblest of Nature's hills. An eminent musician once told me that the folk songs, the songs of the people, are the lifted lowlands out of which the great creations of musical genius soar up to the sky. The ballads of a nation are the lifted lowlands of its poetry. When Gothic Architecture was at the zenith of its achievement, it had behind it, not only the religious faith of the people but also their instinctive art, as expressed in their own handicrafts, and their practical skill.

I shall be reminded that the marvellous culture of Ancient Athens rested on a basis of slave labour. This argument has been overworked by the advocates of an exclusively aristocratic culture. Athenian culture rested on a basis of slave labour in the sense in which the whole Athenian commonwealth

THE SPITALFIELDS WEAVERS

rested on that basis. But to rest on a basis is one thing; to be rooted in it is another. Slaves in antiquity, especially in urban areas, played to a large extent the part which is played to-day by the mechanical contrivances which supply us with water, light, heat, power, drainage and transport, and which count for so much in our social life, that modern culture may almost be said to rest on a basis of applied science and organised machinery. That is why the number of slaves was so large in proportion to the number of enfranchised citizens. The slaves were not, as are our lower orders, an integral part of the social community. Athenian culture may have rested on a basis of slave labour, but it was rooted in the intelligence and good taste of the Athenian *demos*—a *demos* which could listen, with critical appreciation, to the tragedies of Æschylus, Sophocles and Euripides and gaze, with critical appreciation, on the works of Phidias and Praxiteles. "The whole Athenian nation," says Lewes in his *Life of Goethe*, "co-operated with its artists; and this is one cause why Athenian art rose into unsurpassed splendour. Art was not the occupation of a few, ministering to the luxury of a few; it was the luxury of all. Its triumphs were not hidden in galleries and museums; they blazed in the noonday sun; they were admired and criticised by the whole people; and, as Aristotle expressly says, every free citizen was from youth upwards a critic of art." In other words, Athenian culture soared high because, within the limits of the social community, it was broad-based, as broad-based as it was possible for it to be.

When enjoyment of art is a pleasure which the connoisseur keeps to himself, the art in question, or at least that particular development of it, has begun to die, suffocated by its own technique. When the collector appears on the scene the art in question is dead. The intrusion of selfish exclusiveness into art is a sign of incipient decay. For its presence means that the artist has succumbed to the lure of finality and forgotten the call of the infinite, which was his inspiration when his art was young. What the connoisseur enjoys, what the collector prides himself on possessing, is something finished and finite, something which can be weighed and measured, and valued at last in terms of £ s. d. When an art is living and growing, when it is advancing towards its meridian, joy in it is "joy in widest commonalty spread." True art is an adventure into the infinite. As such it ministers to all, appeals to all, and calls for the devotion and service of all.

Our professor will tell us that the masses have no culture and care nothing for it. This may be so to-day. But was it always so? In the Middle Ages and in the earlier of the centuries which we call Modern, the masses, though uneducated and ignorant, had a primitive culture of their own. They had their ballads, their folk songs, their village plays, their morris and other dances, their cottage architecture, their various handicrafts. They

THE SPITALFIELDS WEAVERS

have lost most of these. Let this be fully admitted. But how did they lose them, and who is responsible for the loss? Not the losers themselves. They have been the victims of adverse fate. They have been forcibly decultured, if I may use such a word. But when was this tragedy enacted, and how did it come to pass?

In answer to this question I will tell the story of the Spitalfields Weavers. When I have told it I shall be able to formulate a final objection to our professor's proposal to base the culture of his nation on the virtual enslavement of seven-eighths of its inhabitants. The professor is not alone in the low estimate of his fellow-men which is implicit in his cynical proposal. There is a widespread impression among the upper classes, especially among the persons who pride themselves on their culture, that the working classes have a congenital incapacity for making a profitable use of leisure, and that the shortened hours of work which are now the rule in most industries, will thus be disadvantageous to them as well as to their employers, and that therefore in their own interest as well as in the interest of the whole community they should revert to the longer hours which were usual before and during the war. There is no ground for this ultra-pessimistic assumption. Whippet racing, pigeon fancying, attending football matches, gambling and drinking are not ideal forms of recreation. But if the workers in this and other countries have lost the art of employing leisure, their loss is easily accounted for, and there is no reason why they should not recover what they have lost.

Let us go back a hundred years or so to the days before the poisonous harvest which the Industrial Revolution sowed had fully ripened. From A.D. 1769 to 1824 the wages of the Spitalfields silk weavers were fixed under an Act of Parliament, by the Lord Mayor, Recorder and Aldermen of London, and masters who paid lower or higher wages were liable to a fine of £50. Taking one year with another the wages were high enough to enable the weavers to live in decent comfort and enjoy a reasonable amount of leisure. What use did they make of their leisure? What use were the leisured members of the upper classes at that time making of their super-abundant leisure? For the most part they were engaged in gambling, duelling, dancing, swaggering about at fashionable resorts, hunting, shooting, horse-racing, cock-fighting, illicit love-making, and hard drinking. The recreative activities of the Spitalfields weavers were of a different order from these. An interesting picture of their varied interests was given in 1840 by Edward Church, a solicitor, who had lived for thirty years among them in Spital Square. Of those thirty years, fourteen preceded and sixteen followed the repeal of the Wages Act. The Act applied to London only; and during the whole period from 1810 to 1840 the competition with the London silk industry of the labour-sweating, *rate-aided* silk industries in provincial towns was making itself increasingly felt.

THE SPITALFIELDS WEAVERS

After the repeal of the Act the wages of the Spitalfields weavers fell so low that in order to live they had to work increasingly long hours. Hence the gradual decay of the various societies for mutual instruction and recreation which they had formed. Church describes these societies in the following words:

> The *Spitalfields Mathematical Society* is second in time to the Royal Society and still exists. There was an *Historical Society* which was merged in the *Mathematical Society*. There was a *Flori-cultural Society*, very numerously attended, but now extinct. The weavers were almost the only botanists of their day in the metropolis. They passed their leisure hours, and generally the whole family dined on Sundays, at the little gardens in the environs of London, now mostly built upon, in small rooms about the size of modern omnibuses [1840] with a fireplace at the end. There was an *Entomological Society*, and they were the first entomologists in the kingdom. The Society is gone. They had a *Recitation Society* for Shakespearean readings, as well as reading other authors, which is almost forgotten. They had a *Musical Society*, but this is also gone. They had a *Columbarian Society*, which gave a silver medal as a prize for the best pigeons of the fancy breed. They were great bird-fanciers, and breeders of canaries, many of whom now cheer their quiet hours while at the loom. Their breed of spaniels called Splashers were of the best sporting blood ... . Many of the weavers were Freemasons, but there are now very few left, and these old men. Many of the houses in Spitalfields had porticos with seats at their doors, where the weavers might be seen on summer evenings enjoying their pipes. The porticos have given way to improvements of the pavements.

An idyllic picture this, but as pathetic as it is idyllic. The gradual decay of the once flourishing societies under the inexorable pressure of falling wages and lengthening hours of work, was a veritable tragedy. But the fight of the weavers against adverse fate was not in vain. For in the course of it they showed what the working classes were able to do in the way of recreation and self-education when they had decent wages *and leisure*. In the pre-factory days, when weaving and other industries were carried on in the homes of the workers, the combination of decent wages with leisure was by no means rare. Those who have studied the social and economic life of the eighteenth century tell us that in that age of transition something of the primitive but genuine culture which the lower orders had evolved in the Middle Ages lingered on in the rural and the industrial villages. The freeholders in the former and the homeworkers in the latter, being to some extent their own masters and therefore able to regulate their working hours, still had their folk songs and their morris dances, and could do many things with their hands which they cannot do now. It was in the soil of that primitive culture that the splendid initiative of the Spitalfields weavers may have had its roots. Then came the Industrial Revolution, accompanied in the rural districts by the enclosure of the Common Lands, and in the world of ideas by the rise of political economy, which taught, or was understood to teach, that labour was a commodity to be bought in the cheapest and sold in the dearest market. The joint action of these three movements

THE SPITALFIELDS WEAVERS

reduced the working classes to a state of serfdom and semi-starvation. Wages fell so low that in order to keep body and soul together the labourers, both in town and country, *and their children*, had to work from thirteen to fifteen hours a day. Having no leisure they naturally lost the art of making a profitable use of leisure. Then, to make matters worse, came a wave of puritanical Evangelicalism which swept over the country and carried with it the notion (much favoured by the employers of labour) that all recreation, at any rate on the part of the working classes, was " carnal," and that the harder the poor worked and the less they enjoyed life, the more likely they were to be " saved." At last things came to such a pass that the public-house became the only place of recreation, and drinking the only distraction from the monotony of never-ending and ill-paid toil.

The workers now have reasonably high wages and a fair amount of leisure. What use will they make of the latter? It is possible that at first they will go in with redoubled energy for their favourite amusements — whippet-racing, pigeon fancying, football matches and the rest. And they will probably give more time to gardening, which has, I believe, always attracted them whenever allotments were available. But the need for a higher and wider range of activities will gradually make itself felt. If the workers cannot at once rise to the level of the Spitalfields weavers, the upper classes, who either robbed them of their leisure or acquiesced—with pious resignation—in the robbery, must bear the blame of this. The Spitalfields weavers have given a lead to the workers of to-day, which they will not fail to follow, especially if they have been allowed to have varied interests in their elementary schools, and encouraged to form societies for mutual improvement and amusement in their continuation schools.

For, be it carefully observed, whatever the weavers did in the way of self-education and rational recreation, they did for themselves. There was no one to help them. There was no Board of Education to provide them in their early years with schools and teachers. There were no earnest philanthropists to guide them, when they grew up, into the path of self-development. They sought and found that path for themselves, and they had travelled far along it when loss of leisure, enforced by the threat of starvation, compelled them to quit it. Perhaps one reason why they had travelled so far was that they had found the path and explored it for themselves. Their initiative had not been starved in childhood by a repressive education which left them no room for independent action. And what survived of it had not been extinguished in adult life by that well-meaning but fussy and overofficious philanthropy which postulates the helplessness of the lower orders and then does its best to make them helpless. There is a moral to all this which is so obvious that I will ask the members of this conference to draw it for themselves.

THE SPITALFIELDS WEAVERS

I am perhaps looking far into the future when I say that the workers, when leisure has lost its novelty for them, the novelty which tempts them to misuse it, will follow the lead which the Spitalfields weavers gave a hundred years ago. But I am confident that the time of which I dream will come at last. For, above all, the weavers, now that the story of their doings has been given to the world, have killed the wicked superstition that the working classes have a congenital disinclination and incapacity for self-improvement. They have killed this superstition by proving that it is a superstition, and nothing more. And there was need for it to be killed. When the " masters " in town and country—the millowners, the squires and the farmers—had done their best to debase and brutalise their labourers by persistently over-working and under-paying them, they and the rest of the upper classes—male and female, lay and clerical—had the effrontery to say that the social order, *as it existed then*, had been ordained by God, and in the strength of this self-flattering assumption they turned round upon the victims of their own rapacity and cruelty, and said (as some of them still say) that they were (and are) base-born brutes.

No, the lower strata of society are no more base-born than the higher. Their natural ability is as great. So is their latent capacity for self-sacrifice and disinterested devotion. I do not say that all men are born equal in these respects. I am very sure that they are all born unequal. But I do say most emphatically that we have no evidence that there is any natural inequality between class and class. Professor Cizek, the Viennese art master, the work of whose youthful pupils, now being exhibited in this country and in this town, has astonished and delighted all who have seen it, told one of his interviewers that his best pupils come from the "proletariat": " I would rather have the proletariat child—I would much rather. He has more 'attack' and is less spoiled." In some of our schools original composition in prose and verse is now encouraged by the teachers; and the response which the children are making to this appeal to their creative impulse is on the whole surprisingly good. But the best compositions that I have yet seen come from a higher standard *elementary* school in Yorkshire. And this was not picked work. What was remarkable in that school, as in Professor Cizek's art class, was the extraordinary high level of attainment which the *average* child reached. In each case capacity had been liberated by the skill and sympathy of the teacher,—capacity, the existence of which would have remained unsuspected, had not the teacher, in Professor Cizek's words, taken the lid off instead of clapping it on.

This leads me to state the fifth and last objection to our professor's theory, an objection which is a corollary to and in some sort a restatement of the fourth. Our professor has taken for granted that the masses have a congenital distaste for culture. If I am not mistaken, he has also taken for granted

THE SPITALFIELDS WEAVERS

that they have a congenital incapacity for it. Indeed it is only by adding this assumption to the other that he can attempt to justify his theory. But the second assumption is as baseless as the first. There is reason to believe that the masses, in proportion to their numbers, are by nature as well able to enjoy and appreciate culture as are the more leisured classes, and also as well able to produce and diffuse it; in other words, that they are by nature as well endowed with taste, with talent and, above all, with creative genius. If I cannot prove this statement, I can at least defy its critics to disprove it. There is evidence in support of it. The results of the experiments of Professor Cizek and the gifted teacher of English—experiments which do not stand alone—raise a presumption in its favour. So does the long list of men in all lands and all ages who have risen to greatness in defiance of the many disadvantages of obscure and lowly birth. And the evidence that seems to tell against it is wholly inconclusive, comparison between social stratum and stratum, as regards capacity for culture, being impossible when the facilities for acquiring it are glaringly unequal.

But if the natural capacity of the masses is equal, or even approximately equal, to that of the classes, the loss to culture, owing to its being to a large extent beyond the reach of the former, must be very great. And if our professor could have his way, the loss would be greater still. The masses are perhaps seven times as numerous as the classes.

EDMOND G. A. HOLMES

It follows that if all men, without distinction of class, from the hour of their birth, could have equal opportunities for self-development, we might have eight times as many poets, artists, men of letters, thinkers, historians, pioneers in science, etc., as we have now. And the broader this high plateau of culture, the higher, one might hope, would be the peaks that rose from it as their base.

It is in respect of their social, not of their protoplasmic heritage, of the circumstances of birth, not of birth itself, that the lower classes are less fortunate than the upper. They are born into an environment which is as a rule narrower, ruder, more cramping, more depressing, less stimulating, less inspiring, an environment which cuts them off, in no small measure, from the world's great tradition of art, of letters, of high thinking, of refined and gentle living; an environment which can scarcely fail to stamp its own defects, both positive and negative, on their impressionable hearts during childhood and adolescence. It is for education, first of the child and then of the adolescent, to redress this inequality by giving those who have been less fortunate in their start in life opportunities for all-round self-development. It is for education to lift the average level of the lower social strata, in respect of culture, to the average level of the higher. It is for education to do this, and then to do something more than this. The differences between stratum and stratum in respect of culture (in the true and deep sense of the word) are as nothing compared with the differences in this respect between man as he is and man as he might be. To lead the whole human race, without respect to class, in the direction of its own ideal, is the noblest task that education can set itself. And it is a task which education alone can undertake with any hope of success.

THE CRYSTAL VASE
By Maurice Hewlett

I HAVE often wished that I could write a novel in which, as mostly in life, thank goodness, nothing happens. Jane Austen, it has been objected, forestalled me there, and it is true that she very nearly did—but not quite. It was a point for her art to make that the novel should have form. Form involved plot, plot a logic of events; events—well, that means that there were collisions. They may have been mild shocks, but persons did knock their heads together, and there were stars to be seen by somebody. In life, in a majority of cases, there are no stars, yet life does not on that account cease to be interesting; and even if stars should happen to be struck out, it is not the collision, nor the stars either, which interest us most. No, it is our state of soul, our mental process under the stress which we care about, and as mental process is always going on, and the state of the soul is never the same for two moments together, there is ample material for a novel of extreme interest, which need never finish, which might indeed be as perennial as a daily newspaper or the *Annual Register*. Why is it, do you suppose, that anybody, if he can, will read anybody else's letter? It is because every man-Jack of us lives in a cage, cut off from every other man-Jack; because we are incapable of knowing what is going on in the mind of our nearest and dearest, and because we burn for the assurance we may get by evidence of homogeneity procurable from any human source. Man is a creature of social instinct condemned by his nature to be solitary. Creatures in all outward respects similar to himself are awhirl about him. They cannot help him, nor he them; he cannot even be sure, for all he may assume it, that they share his hope and calling.

> Ensphered in flesh we live and die,
>   And see a myriad souls adrift,
> Our likes, and send our voiceless cry
>   Shuddering across the void: "The truth!
> Succour! The truth!" None can reply.

That is the state of our case. We can cope with mere events, comedy, tragedy, farce. The things that happen to us are not our life. They are imposed upon life, they come and go. But life is a secret process. We only see the accretions.

The novel which I dreamed of writing has recently been done, or rather begun, by Miss Dorothy Richardson. She betters the example of Jane Austen by telling us much more about what seems to be infinitely less, but is not so in reality. She dips into the well whereof Miss Austen skims the surface. She has essayed to report the mental process of a young woman's lifetime from moment to moment. In the course of four, if not five, volumes nothing has happened yet but the death

MAURICE HEWLETT

of a mother and the marriage of a sister or so. She may write forty, and I shall be ready for the forty-first. Mental process, the states of the soul, emotional reaction—these as they are moved in us by other people are Miss Richardson's subject-matter, and according as these are handled is the interest we can devote to her novels. These fleeting things are Miss Richardson's game, and they are the things which interest us most in ourselves, and the things which we desire to know most about in our neighbours.

But, of course, it won't do. Miss Richardson does not, and cannot, tell us all. A novel is a piece of art which does not so much report life as transmute it. She takes up what she needs for her purpose, and that may not be our purpose. And so it is with poetry—we don't go to that for the facts, but for the essence of fact. The poet who told us all about himself at some particular pass would write a bad poem, for it is his affair to transfigure rather than transmute, to move us by beauty at least as much as by truth. What we look for so wistfully in each other is the raw material of poetry. We can make the finished article for ourselves, given enough matter; and indeed the poetry which is imagined in contemplation is apt to be much finer than that which has passed through the claws of prosody and syntax. The fact, to be short with it, is that literature has an eye upon the consumer. Whether it is marketable or not, it is intended for the public. Now no man will undress in public

THE CRYSTAL VASE

with design. It may be a pity, but so it is. Undesignedly, I don't say. It would be possible, I think, by analysis, to track the successive waves of mental process in *In Memoriam*. Again, *The Angel in the House* brought Patmore as near to self-explication as a poet can go. Shakespeare's Sonnets offer a more doubtful field of experiment.

What then? Shall we go to the letter-writers —to Madame de Sévigné, to Gray, to Walpole and Cowper, Byron and Lamb? A letter-writer implies a letter-reader, and just that inadequacy of spoken communication will smother up our written words. Madame de Sévigné must placate her high-sniffing daughter, Gray must please himself; Walpole must at any cost be lively, Cowper must be urbane to Lady Hesketh or deprecate the judgment of the Reverend Mr. Newton. Byron was always before the looking-glass as he wrote; and as for Charles Lamb, do not suppose that he did anything but hide in his clouds of ink. Sir Sidney Colvin thinks that Keats revealed himself in his letters, but I cannot agree with him. Keats is one of the best letter-writers we have; he can be merry, fanciful, witty, thoughtful, even profound. He has a sardonic turn of language hardly to be equalled outside Shakespeare. "Were it in my device, I would reject a Petrarchal coronation—on account of my dying day, and because women have cancers." Where will you match that but from *Hamlet*? But Keats knew himself. "It is a wretched thing to confess, but it is a very fact, that not one word I can utter can be taken for granted as an opinion growing out of my identical Nature." So I find him in his letters, swayed rather by his fancies than his states of soul, until indeed that soul of his was wrung by agony of mind and disease of body. Revelation, then, like gouts of blood, did issue, but of that I do not now write. No man is sane at such a crisis.

Parva componere magnis, there is a letter contained in *The Early Diary of Frances Burney* (ed. Mrs. A. R. Ellis, 1889), more completely apocalyptic than anything else of the kind accessible to me. Its writer was Maria Allen, daughter of Dr. Burney's second wife, therefore half-sister to the charming Burney girls. She was a young lady who could let herself go, in act as well as on paper, and withal, as Fanny judged her, " flighty, ridiculous, uncommon, lively, comical, entertaining, frank, and undisguised "—or because of it—she did contrive to unfold her panting and abounding young self more thoroughly than the many times more expert. You have her here in the pangs of a love-affair, of how long standing I don't know, but now evidently in a bad state of miss-fire. It was to end in elopement, post-chaise, clandestine marriage, in right eighteenth-century. Here is it in an earlier state, all mortification, pouting and hunching of the shoulder. I reproduce it with Maria's punctuation, which shows it to have proceeded, as no doubt she did herself, in gasps:

" I was at the Assembly, forced to go entirely

against my own Inclination. But I always have sacrificed my own Inclinations to the will of other people—could not resist the pressing Importunity of—Bet Dickens—to go—tho' it proved Horribly stupid. I drank tea at the—told old Turner—I was determined not to dance—he would not believe me—a wager ensued—half a crown provided I followed my own Inclinations—agreed—Mr. Audley asked me. I refused—sat still—yet followed my own Inclinations. But four couple began—Martin (c'etait Lui) was there—yet stupid—n'importe—quite Indifferent—on both sides—Who had I—to converse with the whole Evening—not a female friend—none there—not an acquaintance—All Dancing—who then—I've forgot—n'importe—I broke my earring—how—heaven knows—foolishly enough—one can't always keep on the Mask of Wisdom—well n'importe I danced a Minuet à quatre the latter end of the Eve—with a stupid Wretch—need I name him—They danced cotillions almost the whole Night—two sets—yet I did not join them—Miss Jenny Hawkins danced—with who—can't you guess—well—n'importe——"

There is more, but my pen is out of breath. Nobody but Mr. Jingle ever wrote like that; and in so far as Maria Allen may be said to have had a soul, there in its little spasms is the soul of Maria Allen, with all the *malentendus* of the ballroom and all the surgings of a love-affair at cross-purposes thrown in.

MAURICE HEWLETT

As for Fanny Burney's early diary, its careful and admirable editor claims that you have in it " the only published, perhaps the only existing record of the life of an English girl, written of herself in the eighteenth century." I believe that to be true. It is a record, and a faithful and very charming record of the externals of such a life. As such it is, to me, at least, a valuable thing. If it does not unfold the amiable, brisk, and happy Fanny herself, there are two simple reasons why it could not. First, she was writing her journal for the entertainment of old Mr. Crisp of Chessington, the " Daddy Crisp " of her best pages; secondly, it is not at all likely that she knew of anything to unfold. Nor, for that matter, was Fanny herself of the kind that can unfold to another person. Yet there is a charm all over the book, which some may place here, some there, but which all will confess. For me it is not so much that Fanny herself is a charming girl, and a girl of shrewd observation, of a pointed pen, and an admirable gift of mimicry. She has all that, and more—she has a good heart. Her sister Susan is as good as she, and there are many of Susan's letters. But the real charm of the book, I think, is in the series of faithful pictures it contains of the everyday round of an everyday family. Dutch pictures all—passers-by, a knock at the front door, callers—Mr. Young, " in light blue embroidered with silver, a bag and sword, and walking in the rain "; a jaunt to Greenwich, a concert at home—the Agujari in one of her humours; a masquerade—"a very private one, at the house of Mr. Laluze. . . . Hetty had for three months thought of nothing else . . . she went as a Savoyard with a hurdy-gurdy fastened round her waist. Nothing could look more simple, innocent and pretty. My dress was a close pink Persian vest covered with a gauze in loose pleats. . . ." What else? Oh, a visit to Teignmouth—Maria Allen now Mrs. Ruston; another to Worcester; quiet days at King's Lynn, where "I have just finished *Henry and Frances* . . . the greatest part of the last volume is wrote by Henry, and on the gravest of grave subjects, and that which is most dreadful to our thoughts, Eternal Misery. . . ." Terrific novel: but need I go on? There may be some to whom a description of the nothings of our life will be as flat as the nothings themselves—but I am not of that party. The things themselves interest me, and I confess the charm. It is the charm of innocence and freshness, a morning dew upon the words.

The Burneys, however, can do no more for us than shed that auroral dew. They cannot reassure us of our normal humanity, since they needed reassurance themselves.

Where, then, shall we turn? So far as I am aware, to two only, except for two others whom I leave out of account. Rousseau is one, for it is long since I read him, but my recollection is that the *Confessions* is a kind of novel, premeditated, selective, done with great art. Marie Bashkirtseff is another.

MAURICE HEWLETT

I have not read her at all. Of the two who remain I leave Pepys also out of account, because, though it may be good for us to read Pepys, it is better to have read him and be through with it. There, under the grace of God, go a many besides Pepys, and among them every boy who has ever befouled a wall with a stump of pencil. We are left then with one whom it is ill to name in the same fill of the inkpot, "Wordsworth's exquisite sister," as Keats, who saw her once, at once knew her to be.

In Dorothy Wordsworth's journals, you may have the delight of daily intercourse—*famigliarmente discorrendo*—with one of the purest and noblest souls ever housed in flesh; to that you may add the reassurance to be got from word and implication beyond doubt. She tells us much, but implies more. We may see deeply into ourselves, but she sees deeply into a deeper self than most of us can discern. It is not only that, knowing her, we are grounded in the rudiments of honour and lovely living; it is to learn that human life can be so lived, and to conclude that of that at least is the Kingdom of Heaven.

These journals are for fragments only of the years which they cover, and as such exist for Jan.–May, 1798 (Alfoxden); May–Dec., 1800, Oct.–Dec., 1801, Jan.–July, 1802: all these at Grasmere. They have been printed by Professor Knight, and I have the assurance of Mr. Gordon Wordsworth that what little has been omitted is unimportant. Nothing is unimportant to me, and I wish the whole had been given us; but what we have is enough whereby to trace the development of her extraordinary mind and of her power of self-expression. The latter, undoubtedly, grew out of emotion, which gradually culminated until the day of William Wordsworth's marriage. There it broke, and with it, as if by a determination of the will, there the revelation ceased. A new life began with the coming of Mary Wordsworth to Dove Cottage, a life of which Dorothy records the surface only.

The Alfoxden fragment (20th Jan.–22nd May, 1798), written when she was twenty-seven, is chiefly notable for its power of interpreting landscape. That was a power which Wordsworth himself possessed in a high degree. There can be no doubt, I think, that they egged each other on, but I myself should find it hard to say which was egger-on and which the egged. This is the first sentence of it:

20th Jan.—The green paths down the hillsides are channels for streams. The young wheat is streaked by silver lines of water running between the ridges, the sheep are gathered together on the slopes. After the wet dark days, the country seems more populous. It peoples itself in the sunbeams.

Here is one of a few days later:

23rd.—Bright sunshine: went out at 3 o'cl. The sea perfectly calm blue, streaked with deeper colour by the clouds, and tongues or points of sand: on our return of a gloomy red. The sun gone down. The crescent moon, Jupiter and Venus. The sound of the sea distinctly heard on the tops of the hills, which

MAURICE HEWLETT

we could never hear in summer. We attribute this partly to the bareness of the trees, but chiefly to the absence of the singing birds, the hum of insects, that noiseless noise which lives in the summer air. The villages marked out by beautiful beds of smoke. The turf fading into the mountain road.

She handles words, phrases, like notes or chords of music, and never gets her landscape by direct description. One more picture and I must leave it:

26th.— . . . Walked to the top of a high hill to see a fortification. Again sat down to feed upon the prospect: a magnificent scene, *curiously* spread out for even minute inspection, though so extensive that the mind is afraid to calculate its bounds. . . .

Coleridge was with them most days, or they with him. Here is a curious point to note. Dorothy records:

March 7th.—William and I drank tea at Coleridge's. Observed nothing particularly interesting. . . . One only leaf upon the top of a tree—the sole remaining leaf—danced round and round like a rag blown by the wind.

And Coleridge has in *Christabel*:

> The one red leaf, the last of its clan,
> That dances as often as dance it can,
> Hanging so light, and hanging so high,
> On the topmost twig that looks up at the sky.

William, Dorothy, and Coleridge went to Hamburg at the end of that year, but in 1800 the brother and sister were in Grasmere; and the journal, which opens with 14th May, at once betrays the great passion of Dorothy's life:

William and John set off into Yorkshire after dinner at half-past two o'clock, cold pork in their

THE CRYSTAL VASE

pockets. I left them at the turning of the Low-Wood bay under the trees. My heart was so full I could hardly speak to W., when I gave him a farewell kiss. I sate a long time upon a stone at the margin of the lake, and after a flood of tears my heart was easier. The lake looked to me, I know not why, dull and melancholy, and the weltering on the shore seemed a heavy sound. . . . I resolved to write a journal of the time till W. and J. return, and I set about keeping my resolve, because I will not quarrel with myself, and because I shall give William pleasure by it when he comes again. . . .

"Because I will not quarrel with myself"! She is full of such illuminations. Here is another:

Sunday, June 1st.—After tea went to Ambleside round the lakes. A very fine warm evening. Upon the side of Loughrigg *my heart dissolved in what I saw.*

Now here is her account of a country funeral which she reads into, or out of, the countryside:

Wednesday, 3rd Sept.— . . . a funeral at John Dawson's. . . . I was affected to tears while we stood in the house, the coffin lying before me. There were no near kindred, no children. When we got out of the dark house the sun was shining, and the prospect looked as divinely beautiful as I ever saw it. It seemed more sacred than I had ever seen it, *and yet more allied to human life*. I thought she was going to a quiet spot, and I could not help weeping very much. . . .

The italics are mine. William was pleased to call her weeping "nervous blubbering."

And then we come to 1802, the great last year of a twin life; the last year of the five in which those two had lived as one soul and one heart. They were at Dove Cottage, on something under £150 a year. Poems were thronging thick about them; they were living intensely. John was alive. Mary Hutchinson was at Sockburn. Coleridge was still Coleridge, not the bemused and futile mystic he was to become. As for Dorothy, she lives a thing enskied, floating from ecstasy to ecstasy. It is the third of March, and William is to go to London. "Before we had quite finished breakfast Calvert's man brought the horses for Wm. We had a deal to do, pens to make, poems to be put in order for writing, to settle for the press, pack up. . . . Since he left me at half-past eleven (it is now two) I have been putting the drawers in order, laid by his clothes, which he had thrown here and there and everywhere, filed two months' newspapers, and got my dinner, two boiled eggs and two apple tarts. . . . The robins are singing sweetly. Now for my walk. I *will* be busy. I *will* look well, and be well when he comes back to me. O the Darling! Here is one of his bitter apples, I can hardly find it in my heart to throw it into the fire. . . . I walked round the two lakes, crossed the stepping-stones at Rydalefoot. Sate down where we always sit. I was full of thought of my darling. Blessings on him." Where else in our literature will you find mood so tender, so intimately, so delicately related?

A week later, and William returned. With him, it seems, her descriptive powers. "Monday morning—a soft rain and mist. We walked to Rydale for letters. The Vale looked very beautiful in excessive simplicity, yet at the same time, uncommon obscurity. The church stood alone, mountains behind. The meadows looked calm and rich, bordering on the still lake. Nothing else to be seen but lake and island." Exquisite landscape. For its like we must go to Japan. Here is another. An interior. It is the 23rd of March, " about ten o'clock, a quiet night. The fire flickers, and the watch ticks. I hear nothing save the breathing of my beloved as he now and then pushes his book forward, and turns over a leaf. . . ." No more, but the peace of it is profound, the art incomparable.

In April, between the 5th and 12th, William went into Yorkshire upon an errand which she knew and dreaded. Her trouble makes the words throb.

Monday, 12th. . . . The ground covered with snow. Walked to T. Wilkinson's and sent for letters. The woman brought me one from William and Mary. It was a sharp windy night. Thomas Wilkinson came with me to Barton and questioned me like a catechiser all the way. Every question was like the snapping of a little thread about my heart. I was so full of thought of my half-read letter and other things. I was glad when he left me. Then I had time to look at the moon while I was thinking of my own thoughts. The moon travelled through the clouds, tinging them yellow as she passed along, with two stars near her, one larger than the other. . . . At this time William, as I found the next day, was riding by himself between Middleham and Barnard Castle.

I don't know where else to find the vague

torment of thought, its way of enhancing colour and form in nature, more intensely observed. Next day: "When I returned *William* was come. *The surprise shot through me.*" This woman was not so much poet as crystal vase. You can see the thought cloud and take shape.

The twin life was resumed for yet a little while. In the same month came her descriptions of the daffodils in Gowbarrow Park, and of the scene by Brothers Water, which prove to anybody in need of proof that she was William's well-spring of poesy. Not that the journal is necessarily involved. No need to suppose that he even read it. But that she could make him see, and be moved by, what she had seen is proved by this: "17th.— . . . I saw a robin chasing a scarlet butterfly this morning"; and "Sunday, 18th.— . . . William wrote the poem on *The Robin and the Butterfly.*" No, beautiful beyond praise as the journals are, it is certain that she was more beautiful than they. And what a discerning, illuminative eye she had! "As I lay down on the grass, I observed the glittering silver line on the ridge of the backs of the sheep, owing to their situation respecting the sun, which made them look beautiful, but with something of strangeness, like animals of another kind, as if belonging to a more splendid world. . . ." What a woman to go a-gipsying through the world with!

Then comes the end. . . . "Thursday, 8th July.— . . . In the afternoon, after we had talked a little, William fell asleep. I read *The*

THE CRYSTAL VASE

Winter's Tale; then I went to bed but did not sleep. The swallows stole in and out of their nest, and sat there, *whiles* quite still, *whiles* they sung low for two minutes or more at a time, just like a muffled robin. William was looking at *The Pedlar* when I got up. He arranged it, and after tea I wrote it out—280 lines. . . . The moon was behind. . . . We walked first to the top of the hill to see Rydale. It was dark and dull, but our own vale was very solemn—the shape of Helm Crag was quite distinct, though black. We walked backwards and forwards on the White Moss path; there was a sky like white brightness on the lake. . . . O beautiful place! Dear Mary, William. The hour is come. . . . I must prepare to go. The swallows, I must leave them, the wall, the garden, the roses, all. Dear creatures, they sang last night after I was in bed; seemed to be singing to one another, just before they settled to rest for the night. Well, I must go. Farewell."

Next day she set out with William to meet her secret dread, knowing that life in Rydale could never be the same again. Wordsworth married Mary Hutchinson on the 4th October, 1802. The secret is no secret now, for Dorothy was a crystal vase.

PLATO AS A NOVELIST

By Vida D Scudder

How far behind us seem the days when the future author of *Adam Bede* wrote sedately to a youthful friend that she read no novels, because "the weapons of the Christian warfare were never sharpened at the forge of Romance"! Whatever be true of Christian warfare and its weapons, novels are nowadays a necessary and wholesome part of everyone's daily life. Did they serve no other purpose, they afford an invaluable gymnastic of the sympathies. Reading them, we acquire with minimum effort a broadening of our affections, a liking for all sorts and conditions of people, including not a few—crooks, drunkards, fools even,—from whom in real life we should turn with disgust and distaste. If we moderns are growing more inwardly democratic, if we take life with more emotional versatility and humorous tolerance than our forbears, we owe the gain less to our political institutions than to our excellent habit of indiscriminate novel reading. Wiseacres may bid us devote our whole mind to Bergson. Him we shall not neglect. But let us also insist on

PLATO AS A NOVELIST

the advantage to our manners and our morals of familiarity with *Havoc*, *A Millionaire Baby*, and *The Tu-Tze's Tower*.

Yet there is a melancholy fact which we cannot escape. As people grow older, they get fussy about their fiction. Reproachfully, despondently, middle age finds that it has lost the delectable power of youth to enjoy anything in story form. The mysteries seem set in pattern, and flat when solved. The princesses of Graustein have no more attraction than summer girls in a tennis court. The latest flights of psychic aeroplanes lift us away from earth if you will, but into peculiarly vacuous mid-air. And the grim tales of mean streets revolt like a stroll through the slums in hot weather.

This I submit is the moment for Plato. Not Plato the philosopher. Such a gentleman may exist, spinning an intricate spider web of dialectic, along whose tenuous gossamers the daring intellect darts insecurely outward towards its elusive prey, a conclusion. This subtle personage is no hammock companion. Plato the novelist is our man; writer of fiction bathed in the immortal dew of the world's dawning; magician who evokes for us the moving-picture of the most fascinating society ever known; master delineator of the weaknesses and the loveliness of men. Tell me if you will of a Plato wise in archetypal ideas, concerned with the relations of knowledge and virtue, keen on pursuit of the perfect state. Him I seek not in the summer noons, —nay, but the witty satirist, the lofty lover, the creator of that most vivid character in the world's fiction, who is the friend of Crito and Agathon, the adorer of Charmides, the beloved by Alcibiades. With this Plato I can keep delightful fellowship, whithersoever he may lead.

Nowhere shall I find more variety. Does my palate crave comic salt? Here is *Euthydemus*, bubbling over with pure mischief, which finally breaks into farce roaring as that of *The Pickwick Papers*, when the two Sophists, twisted up by Socrates to assert that everything is what it isn't, are greeted with a tumult of glee. Is high romance to my taste? Here it weaves spells true as in Shakespeare's sonnets; for these Dialogues abound with sentiment of every shade, and at the same banquet we may encounter passion most lofty and most base, listening at will to Diotima or to Alcibiades. Do we find light society sketches more to our mind than confidences so searching? The early Dialogues, *Lysis*, *Charmides*, *Laches*, and the rest, aim at nothing and hit it as inconclusively as modern realism, yet are felicitous as Jane Austen in echoing the chit-chat of the town and the evanescent moods of well-bred people. Where is a more amusing scene than the opening of the *Protagoras*? Where a sweeter idyll than the picture of Socrates in the *Phædrus*, dabbling his toes in the brook under the plane-tree, as he spins lazy yarns about that fair creature Psyche, and ends with an exquisite prayer to Pan? The aeroplane of the *Timæus* sweeps us into planetary space more effectively than that of Marie Corelli; *Phædo* and the *Apology* purify by pity and terror as only great tragedy can do.

The beauty of the art is that none of these types is produced mechanically after the modern fashion. Life in its entirety is in Plato behind each mode of life. Through the gayest persiflage plays suddenly high passion for the argument. Presto! Greek worldly wisdom inhibits with salutary jest some imaginative flight. Do not tell me that I am reading the man who has infected the generations with a microbe tempting them to prefer dream to fact. My Plato is obsessed by desire for experience, singularly alive to the concrete, fascinated by the stir and movement of very life. He is the match of Dickens for portraiture, of Meredith for dramatic dialogue, of Browning for situation. With Balzac or Tolstoi, he is competent to quicken us by the spectacle of existence, now to tragic passion, now to the laughter of the gods.

We may be pardoned for finding the dialectic stiff, and for offering our meek "Certainly" at intervals with Laches or Nicias, not quite sure to what we are assenting, but either because we want to please Socrates, or because the maddening old man will tease us worse if we contradict him. Let us forget the talk, think of the talkers, and give thanks for the men and manners that live for us in these pages. A sense of solid reality is the ultimate impression imparted to the literary mind by this greatest of the world's idealists.

Socrates is the centre of the group, of course,

and we all think we know Socrates, though we are mistaken. But why ignore the Athenians who gather round him? How they stand out, the child and the citizen, the soldier and the actor, the academic dignitary, the plain man on the street! No dummies they, giving absent assent to the great teacher. Most are defined as to aspect with a few perfect touches, each speaks in character. In the dramatically vital dialogue, the very manner in which they take refutation, the quality of their agreement—now sullen, now eager, now careless, now thoughtful—sets them before us with high imaginative art. And how admirably are they introduced, in those lovely settings which give us perhaps our most vivid knowledge of Greek life! Especially in the minor Dialogues, which are rather tentative *jeux d'esprit* than philosophical discussions, the argument does not pretend to get anywhere. It chases its own tail and drops like a tired kitten on the spot where it began. But meantime we are seeing life, we are meeting Greeks, and we do not care a rap whether or no we succeed in defining friendship or temperance or courage. It is more important to chat with the boy Charmides, to enjoy his choice manners and his rare beauty, and inhale the aroma of his delightful youth.

Socrates, in this Dialogue, is just back from military service at Potidæa, where he has borne hardship and danger stolidly, as Alcibiades shall one day tell us. Now he is hungry for civilisation: the hum in the palæstra is delectable to him. We listen for a few minutes to greetings, and the pleasant gossip of the town. It must be acknowledged that Socrates asks about "the present state of philosophy," as one might inquire into politics after absence in foreign parts; but presently with equal interest he is asking about the season's "buds." These—we are in Greece—are the lads just reaching manhood. Are any of them remarkable, he wants to know, for beauty or sense? And just then the merry troop appears, making a great din, one of them, Charmides, easily the most beautiful. "I must admit," says Socrates, "that I was quite astonished at his beauty and stature. All the world seemed to be enamoured of him. Amazement and confusion reigned when he entered. All the boys, even to the very least child, turned and looked at him, as if he were a statue. Chærephon called to me and said:

"'What do you think of him, Socrates? Has he not a beautiful face? But you would think nothing of his face if you could see his naked form.'

"'By Heracles,' I said, 'there never was such a paragon, if he has only one other slight addition.'

"'What is that?' said Critias.

"'If he has a noble soul; and being of your house, Critias, he may be expected to have this.'

"'He is fair and good within as he is without,' said Critias.

"'Shall we ask him, then,' I said, 'to show us, not his body, but his soul? He is just of an age when he will like to talk.'"

Hard to surpass in modern fiction, that bit of dialogue! Here is full Greece: delight in beauty of form as of countenance; swift courtesy; the Socratic love of loveliness within—" Is not the wiser always the fairer, sweet friend?" asks the sage in another connection; and finally the unquenchable zest for conversation.

What interests Socrates just now is not an abstract question, but a charming boy. He proceeds to invent topics, that he may savour the soul of Charmides. First they talk a little about a headache that bothers the lad—ailments, then as now, forming a convenient introductory theme. And Christian Science would seem to be less original than it supposes, for we find Socrates remarking that Charmides can get rid of his headache easily if he will cure his soul " by the use of certain charms, and these charms are fair words." All very well, but they soon grow bored over Charmides' headache, and cast about for another subject. Temperance will do; what does Charmides think of temperance? He is a remarkably temperate lad, by the way, remarks his relative, Critias, taking no pains to lower his voice.

Charmides blushes—his blushes come readily—at this blatant praise. Then, after some hesitation he feels his way till he says that temperance is quietness. Not a bad answer, surely—one well befitting a young Greek gentleman. Socrates, however, though pleased, points out that a sluggish man is not necessarily a temperate one, and that energetic actions are usually better than slow, quiet ones; in a word, that scientific efficiency does not preclude temperance. Greek standards are not so far from modern, we perceive. Charmides tries again, frank ingenuousness and good breeding in his every word: May not temperance be modesty? Then Socrates, with Critias to help, gets seriously to work: the trail may lead in a circle, but to pursue it is great sport, and his object, the enjoyment of Charmides in his lovely youth, has been fully attained.

Lysis is younger than Charmides; he and his chum, Menexenus, are little fellows, hardly beyond childhood. A bigger lad, one Hippothales, has what in college parlance would be termed a " crush " on Lysis; we are in that Greek world where romance lives from man to man. Socrates will show Hippothales the best way to win the boy's affections. At least so he pretends; what he is really after is the pleasure of converse with an awakening mind. How to get at Lysis? Hippothales says that if only Socrates will sit down and begin to talk, the boy will be sure to come, and so it happens. There has been a sacrifice, and all the boys are dressed in white. They are playing a game, taking their dice out of little wicker baskets; small Lysis, crowned with a wreath and fair as a vision, is looking on. Presently he begins to glance around, timidly but wistfully, at Socrates chatting in his quiet corner. Soon his friend Menexenus joins the group, and then Lysis picks up courage to come too—sentimental Hippothales, whom the lad evidently does not like, hiding out of the way. It is a pretty scene, and the talk is equally pretty, though desultory enough on the surface. Anyone who wants an example of a grown-up mind adapting itself wisely and tenderly to childhood, might well turn to it:

"I dare say, Lysis, that your father and mother love you very much?"

"That they do," he said.

"And that they would wish you to be perfectly happy?"

"Yes."

"But do you think that anyone is happy who . . . cannot do what he likes?"

"I should think not indeed," he said. . . .

"Do your father and your mother, then, permit you to do what you like, and never rebuke or hinder you?"

"Yes indeed, Socrates, there are a great many things which they hinder me from doing."

So Lysis has to tackle some hard thinking—yet thinking quite within the compass of a little chap. He enjoys the talk hugely, and wants his friend to share it. "In a childish and affectionate manner," he whispers in Socrates' ear: "Do, Socrates, tell Menexenus what you have been telling me." Once he interrupts: "I am sure that we have been wrong, Socrates." "And he blushed at his own words, as if he had not intended to speak; but the words escaped him involuntarily in his eagerness."

PLATO AS A NOVELIST

Before the talk is over, all concerned know a good deal more than they did about friendship and other important matters—though as for definitions, on which Socrates is daft, they have not reached any. Is friendship based on contrast or similarity of temperament? they wonder, and we are wondering yet. Who knows? They might have decided, or even have reached a definition, had it not been for the tutors. But these break in "like an evil apparition," very cross because it is so late; and though the talkers drive them off, they keep on shouting at their charges till they force them to start for home.

Endearing and beautiful youths like Charmides and Lysis hold a position of central importance throughout the Platonic tales. We know how Socrates loved them, and remember that his fascination over them was a cause of his death. Yet if the Dialogues breathe this ecstatic joy in youth for youth's sake, they are also full of sly delight in noting the humours of grown men. Crito, Socrates' special friend, is an old man, wealthy, dignified, not at all clever. One wonders what he got from lifelong converse with the deepest mind in Greece. Socrates is fond of his company, tells him merry tales like that of the *Euthydemus*; it is to Crito that he addresses his last words. The figure is always respectfully and tenderly touched. So is that of gentle old Lysimachus, who has never heard of Socrates, but has a high regard for Socrates' father. Another old man is Protagoras the Sophist, an academic type cleverly sketched: honest, weighty, a copious lecturer, presenting with facile sonority the truth of the past, and a little fussed and cross under the impact of the truth of the future.

Plato gives us men of action, too. There are the soldiers, Laches and Nicias, who seek a just idea of courage to impart to the rising generation. Laches is a blunt man, annoyed that he cannot express himself: " I fancy I do know the nature of courage," he complains, " but somehow or other she has slipped away from me, and I cannot tell her nature." He considers privately that " the examination of such niceties " as definitions is no suitable employment for a statesman or a soldier. Still he gets a little way when, from satisfaction with the remark that a courageous man is one who does not run away, he discovers with hardly any help that " courage is the endurance of the soul." However, Nicias has to give him yet more hints —ill-fated Nicias, who is shown as one of the most thoughtful people in Plato, hardly inferior to Socrates himself in insight. Was the reflective turn of mind, such an asset to the man, a disadvantage to the soldier?

Other types are the broad-minded physician Eryximachus and Ion the actor — the purely emotional man, this last, a-quiver over his own recitations. Socrates is particularly felicitous with Ion, who avows that there is no part of Homer on which he does not speak well, and that he feels rapt out of himself when he recites, but strange to say, is inclined to be sleepy when anyone else recites from another poet. Socrates, who depreciates himself pleasantly as " a common man who only speaks the truth," treats him gently: tells him that he is quite mad, and when Ion, though acquiescent, is a little subdued, proceeds to say that Homer and all the great imaginations were mad likewise, and that inspiration is none the worse for being irrational, but rather the better; and we leave Ion as pleased and bewildered as M. Jourdain. It is a very amusing dialogue.

Some of Plato's *dramatis personæ* are dull, some slow, some simple-minded; yet on the whole they are amazingly attractive. He shows us no villains. Nevertheless there are shadows, firmly if delicately touched, in his picture. No fierce denunciation—that was not the style of Plato, or his master—but an inexorable trick of letting the shallow, fanatical, or cruel man speak for himself. There is Anytus, for example, in the *Meno*. It is worth while to study Anytus, for he is to be one of Socrates' chief accusers. His inimitable responses, few and brief, illuminate him for ever.

Socrates praises him warmly when he first appears: " There is Anytus sitting by us; he is the person whom we should ask. In the first place, he is the son of a wealthy and wise father, and he is a well-conditioned, modest man, not insolent or overbearing or annoying; moreover, he has given his son a good education." All this appears to be true; it is persons like Anytus who usually put to death Socrates and Jesus. Anytus gives placid acquiescence to the course of the argument till it touches the concrete; then he flares up. This happens to be at a mention of the Sophists. Socrates is mildly surprised; he reasons with Anytus: Can the men whom everyone considers so wise be really out of their minds, as Anytus hints? But Anytus is not a reasoning being. "Out of their minds!" he cries. "No, Socrates, the young men who gave their money to them are out of their minds, and their relatives and guardians who entrusted them to their care were still more out of their minds." What irony, that Socrates should have first incurred this man's suspicions and rage on behalf of the Sophists! For we know that Socrates was not over-fond of the Sophists himself. But how human it all is, and how prone Anytus still is to raise the angry cry, "Out of their minds!" against those with whom he disagrees!

"Has any of the Sophists wronged you, Anytus?" . . .

"No, indeed; neither I nor any of my belongings has ever had, nor would I suffer them to have anything to do with them." . . .

"Then, my dear friend, how can you know whether a thing is good or bad, of which you are wholly ignorant?"

"Quite well. I am quite sure that I know what manner of men these are, whether I know them or not."

Anytus is quite sure still, and he writes for almost every newspaper in the country; his violent talk, charged with prejudice and animosity, greets us in every haunt of men. For Anytus is a "stand-patter"—modest, well-conditioned Anytus, who educates his sons so carefully. "If you won't trust the Sophists, to whom do you look for guidance?" asks Socrates; and Anytus gives the unvarying answer of his caste: "Any Athenian gentleman" taken at random will, so he asserts, do perfectly well. But these gentlemen—did they grow of themselves? Socrates must know; and Anytus, impatiently satisfied, returns the immortal answer: "I imagine that they learned of the previous generation of gentlemen."

It is of no use, Socrates; you might as well leave Anytus alone. But Socrates does not leave him alone, thereby, were safety dear, making a vast mistake. He plays gadfly till he stings the poor, comfortable man past endurance. So Anytus breaks into open rage: accuses Socrates—and again the stand-patter's complaint of the radical sounds queerly familiar—of "speaking evil of men," and utters a veiled threat, sinister enough in the light of the outcome. Socrates dismisses him with a touch of cool contempt, unusual in the suavest of adversaries, who generally coaxes his most irritated antagonists back into the trail of the argument; then turns to point out to the more responsive Meno the unconventionality of virtue, and its immediate character, derived from no tradition, not even that of the gentlemen of Athens. For with subtle instinct for dramatic contrast, Plato includes in this Dialogue that famous scene in which the independent intuition of truth is illustrated by the power of Meno's boy-slave to prove a geometrical proposition.

Nothing could be more natural, more unstudied, than all this talk. It has the desultory wavering of life itself. Of conversation, that crux of the novelist, Plato is past-master; one must turn to Meredith or Anatole France to find his equal. His dialogue makes the ordinary talk, say of the people in Mrs. Humphry Ward, appear soggy with that curse of art, the obvious. There is never too much flour in Plato's baking; and his deft touch is one reason why we rank him among the poets, "light, winged, and holy." He catches the words as they fly, and though they seem to flutter vaguely like butterflies, they are really driving straight like a flight of migrating birds for a goal beyond the horizon.

However, it is to be remembered that Plato had an advantage over modern writers, for he had Greece to present and Athenians for his characters. The fine art of social intercourse is here brought to its last point of perfection. Men are thinking—everybody, except perhaps Anytus, is thinking in Plato—though, being human, they tend to think overmuch the thoughts of other people; but they are never thinking alone. The intellectual life in Greece is a social and not a solitary pursuit. That is why Plato is a great novelist as well as a philosopher. This society is worth reading about, moreover, quite apart from its brains, for the mere charm of its manners, a charm unsurpassed. When Aristodemus appears uninvited at the banquet, how graciously does Agathon put him at his ease! What pretty compliments they pay one another, how generously they admire each other's excellencies, what capital and witty jokes they crack! Never do we pass our time in vulgar company; we are aristocrats in every sense. We move on principle only in the best circles—and how very good they are!

Socrates revels in this society, for he, too, is the most sociable of men. Like Dr. Johnson, whom he much resembles, he takes unfeigned interest in all the little affairs of the town; especially is he quite at home in that perennial topic of conversation, the psychology of the affections. He likes a gossip as well as any man, and has a marvellous catholic taste in his choice of associates. It is entertaining to study him through his reaction on people. Browning did not invent the oblique method of showing character in *The Ring and the Book*. Courteous old Lysimachus, who does not move in intellectual circles, invites Socrates to call because he is the son of his father. The soldier Laches knows him only as a man of action, and has sincere regard for him. Bit by bit, we get a feeling for the man himself. A quick man, intolerant of stupidity, yet helped to patient self-control by the rare, divine instinct of the teacher; taking his revenge in that irony that baffles and allures the ages, an irony of which his successors—Rabelais,

Swift, Arnold—have never quite caught the secret. He never lays down the law, he never loses his grip. Yet one sees that people have one trick that tries him almost past endurance, the inveterate habit of defining by the concrete instance. "Courage is not running away from your post," says Laches. "Temperance is doing things orderly," says Charmides. And Euthyphro, whom we shall meet presently, caps the climax of this kind of definition when he gravely announces: "Virtue is doing as I am doing." But Socrates never snubs one of them; with infinite forbearance he leads them on. Terrible tease, superb old man, who loves the argument, as argument, tenaciously, yet is capable of turning round with splendid inconsistency and "believing where he has not proved"! What a picture! But if we talk of Socrates, we shall never stop. The portrait is literally incomparable; nothing has ever approached it.

So is Plato realist of the realists. Yet at times we leave Greece behind us and below. We watch the soul putting forth her wings, or the chariot of humanity thundering on its perilous way, or the strange life of "earth-born men"; and find ourselves at the fountain-head of the imaginative literature of Europe. Plato the myth-maker gives us more direct narrative than Plato the realist; and his myths, whether in the *Timæus*, the *Phædrus*, or the *Symposium*, are in purest romantic tone. All dreamers have dreamed these dreams after him. Yet from the starry flights through which he bears us we return with pleasure to Greek life. We are glad to know that Socrates held high converse on the passions with Diotima, the priestess, in those mysterious interviews that suggest the very quintessence of romance; for our part, we are well content with the society of the pompous Protagoras and the absurd Euthydemus, of Euthyphro the prig, and fair Agathon, most winning of hosts, of little Lysis, and the rest; with the walk, the palæstra, the beloved scenes through which moves a spirit in Silenus mask, at once their representative and their destroyer. Even in Plato, realism wins out in the long run.

Mastery over dialogue, over characterisation, setting, romantic invention—these are great assets for a novelist. Plato has one more, perhaps greater: unfailing instinct for the dramatic. True, there is as little formal plot as in those admirable intimations concerning M. Bergeret; but there is an immense amount of drama, so to speak, in solution. In the undercurrent of the dialogue, things are constantly happening to people. Relations of affection and hate develop, mature, decay; minds are brought into ever-shifting connections with each other and with ideas. If there is no plot, at least the feeling for situation is strong. Who can forget that dining-hall where Socrates is found at dawn prophesying Shakespeare to the sleepy Aristophanes and Agathon; or the prison where disciples gather around an old man chafing his leg; or the judgment hall, where Socrates, far from keeping august silence as did a

VIDA D. SCUDDER

Greater brought to judgment, pours forth marvellous words for the last time?

Perhaps the most poignant situation just precedes these last. Socrates, awaiting trial in that familiar porch to the temple of King Archon, near which he had once held pleasant converse with young Charmides, encounters Euthyphro the pious soothsayer, to whom he begins to talk with his usual friendly cheer. Socrates is accused by one Meletus, a young man he hardly knows, who " has a beak," it seems, and " long, straight hair, and a beard that is ill-grown." Euthyphro, on the contrary, is an accuser; the man whom he accuses is his own father, arraigned by him on a charge of murder. Socrates' spontaneous start of shocked surprise, his horrified remarks to the complacent Pharisee clinging to the letter of the law, reveal with flashing clarity, as they were meant to do, the deep devoutness and innate reverence for the past of the man to be put to death by respectable Athens for a free-thinker and a corrupter of youth. " Virtue is doing as I am doing "! Or, if you please, men learn their standards " from the preceding generations of gentlemen "! " Neither," says Socrates sternly. Between the arrogant self-confidence of Euthyphro and the conventionality of Anytus, he holds sensitive balance, difficult and just.

Socrates was executed, of course. The *Euthyphro* serves as prelude to the sure tragedy towards which the undercurrent has been setting from the first. For here is the final greatness of Plato's superb historic romance; one tense conflict is in progress from first to last. We discover this gradually, and do not quite understand the situation till all is over. Then, ah! then, looking back, we realise that there has been a plot after all. Over that exquisite youth on which the high lights carefully fall, that youth so delicately presented, so passionately wooed, the world of Athens wedded to its smooth tradition, and the man intent upon the naked truth, must wrestle to the death. These protagonists are shown with a composed mastery of art. The artist's dispassionate sympathy reveals without partisanship the animus of both, as well as that of the onlookers, who are presented with unrivalled finesse.

For there is no mechanical villainy about this Athenian world that kills Socrates. It is admirable in its way. Its conception of a gentleman has never been equalled. Its sense of *noblesse oblige* is strong. We have noted its perfect manners, its gracious charm. Moreover, it is far from being consciously materialised. These noble citizens have the personal beauty and the delight in physical activities of Arnold's barbarians; but show at first sight none of the imperviousness to ideas which he attributes to the class. Quite the contrary. They flock to their lectures and concerts. They prefer after-dinner speeches to music and wine; and their speeches are concerned, not with programmes, as too often befalls us moderns, but with ideas. They think they want to think, these supple-minded Greeks. "Let us follow the argument," they are always blithely saying, " whithersoever it may lead us." As Hippothales says, "Their entertainment is conversation," and the zest of this good talk lives down the ages. It touches with impartial cheer on social justice, philology, military tactics, mysticism, ethics, poetry, small quibbles, and large issues. How well, as a rule, good breeding checks their eagerness, how anxiously they consider the best methods of education, how solicitous they are about the beautiful-and-the-good! And how enthusiastic about great minds! When Protagoras comes to Athens, Hippocrates rushes before daybreak to announce the event; has to feel around in the dark for Socrates' trucklebed; and Socrates has all the trouble in the world persuading him to wait for light before they seek the presence of the sage. He is quite in the fashion, if we may judge from the cross servant who bangs the door in their faces, he is so tired of opening it to seekers. In breadth of outlook, in culture, in lively charm and noble seriousness, this is the very society in which we should all like to live.

And Socrates? Well, Socrates certainly is exasperating to a degree. There is that Silenus aspect of his, when he jeers with such gusto at things we hold sacred. And then we never know whether he is in earnest or not. And he is for ever putting us in the wrong, when we know and he knows that we are in the right. A horrid habit! It undermines our good practical pragmatism, and prevents us from getting a living. Society is bound to put the man to death who allows it no assumptions. It is morally immodest, so Anytus is convinced, to insist like that on pulling off Truth's last garment. Then he is always so maddeningly good-natured! And the vicious fascination of the man! There is youth, adorable, expectant youth, wistfully waiting to be led in that appointed way of honourable, safe tradition in which we are its precursors and natural guides; and there is Socrates, always luring it into untried trails! Can we allow his anarchical force to have its way? Oh, we remember it too well! We are older now, but we too have felt that magic. We know how that voice lured us, how we were be-spelled by the keen wit, the merry word, the ironic play that so easily put our elders to the blush, the delusive sympathy with our interests; how we had glimpses of a far skyey country where the eternal were, which made the streets of Athens flat and dull. Nor have we ever been quite satisfied since, grave citizens though we be, in our function of carrying on the state with due regard to the proprieties. It is all the fault of Socrates! Away with this agitator, this impious person, this corrupter of youth!

For Socrates had been teaching in Athens a long time, and the youths whom he had charmed and wooed, connived when they grew up at killing him Unlike Jesus, whose ministry was brief, though we do not know its exact duration, Socrates had his full, free chance at winning men. And he made a failure at it. Some of his most important pupils —Alcibiades, Charmides, Critias—turned out badly, and the Athenians did not forget it. Most of the others deserted him. Was it that he was on the wrong tack, after all, in trying to make man cultivate virtue by the means of knowledge? Was it that the times were not ripe? At all events, he was much alone at the last. Besides old, faithful Crito, there was a very small group in that prison. Youth had deserted him; tradition had won the day. So he drank his poison—not sorry, one surmises, despite all his cheery love of this good world, to try the great adventure; and the proprieties were left in possession of youth, the forever desired. They usually are, for that matter; this dogged struggle for possession of the future is actual to-day as in Athens, renewed from generation to generation, never lost, never won. Socrates is among us still: always worsted, never disposed of, albeit in our democratic days his spirit is diffused, and must be sought at diverse points of collective experience, rather than in one great figure. And the compositions which show him in his Greek dress moving through that vital and charming society are immortal fiction, not only because they have such rare power to enlarge our sympathies, but because at bottom they present persistent fact.

A RARE TRAVELLER: W. H. HUDSON [1]
By Ernest Rhys

PICTURESQUE topographers and guides to famous places are many. The real discoverers and born naturalists, able to make a country new and wonderful even to the people who have lived in it all their lives, are few at the best of times.

It was the author of *The Paradox Club* who first announced, some years ago, a traveller from South America who had rediscovered Britain. The traveller's name recalled Hudson's Bay and Henry Hudson the Navigator; but his own initials were W. H. and his country was Guayana. To that side of the world, after writing several books about the wilds of London, Sussex, Wilts, Hampshire and Cornwall, Hudson later returned in his unfinished autobiography—*Far Away and Long Ago*. A strange book, as biographies and autobiographies go, treating of nature, human nature, and aspects of life that to-day are often left out of the reckoning, its pages recall some of the earlier books that made its writer known—*Idle Days in Paraguay, The Naturalist in La Plata, South American Sketches,*

[1] The news of W. H. Hudson's death came as this book was going to press; and it was decided to add this tribute to his memory at the close of a volume in which he had been enlisted as a living contributor.

The Purple Land that England Lost, and the perfect little Indian romance, *Green Mansions*, which is in its wild disguise personal too.

The spell of these early South American adventures was so strong and the vision of the world they unfolded so remarkable, that originally they left one wishing almost that the writer would write only of Guayana and the neighbouring lands. But another and older instinct was in his blood, which led him over to this country, and in his English adventures he fully kept his sense of discovery. He described them like a man coming fresh to the scene, while yet feeling the place association that usually comes only with old acquaintance.

This dual interest much increases the effect of his writing. In "The Shepherd of the Downs" he looked on that Sussex country with the eyes of an heir to an old estate, back from exile. But the land of his birth is still in his mind, and every wilder aspect of the one calls up the spirit and the colour of the other. So Wiltshire and Guayana were both in a way mother-earth to him; the South Downs remind him of La Plata, Paraguay and the Banda Oriental, and behind the scenes described in his English pages loom up the deserts and splendours of the new world seen from the top of Ytaioa. In Sussex a day on Kingston Hill (near Lewes) does the trick:

> The wide extent of unenclosed and untilled earth, its sunburnt colour and its solitariness, when no person was in sight; the vast blue sky, with no mist or cloud on it; the burning sun and wind, and the

sight of thousands upon thousands of balls or stars of down, reminded me of old days on horseback on the open pampa—an illimitable waste of rust-red thistles, and the sky above covered with its million floating flecks of white.

By this reversion and his power of bringing an appreciable strangeness into a familiar bit of landscape, he expresses in a fashion peculiar to himself what we may call the primitive colours of the English uplands.

His feeling for them was that of a countryman who was yet a far traveller, a great naturalist, an artist in wild life. To him any scene where there was room, open sky and plenty of wing-space, was haven enough, though to others it seemed treeless and uninviting. He took a place like Winterbourne Bishop—the village without any ivied relic or new hotel to attract the tourist—and make it into the mirror of that place-memory which haunts us like a repeated dream. He could take a tree, as in *El Ombú*, and make it reveal life upon life, generation after generation, in the story it tells. The result is one only attained by an uncommon conjunction of the right subject and the fit man to deal with it.

The actual narrator in *El Ombú* is a Spanish-American exile; and something of a Spanish gravity in the style much enhances the narrative illusion:

Do you hear the mangangá, the carpenter bee, in the foliage over our heads? Look at him, like a ball of shining gold among the green leaves, suspended in one place, humming loudly. Ah, señor, the years that are gone, the people that have lived and died, speak to me thus audibly when I am sitting here by myself. These are memories; but there are other things that come back to us from the past; I mean ghosts. Sometimes, at midnight, the whole tree, from its great roots to its topmost leaves, is seen from a distance shining like white fire. What is that fire, seen of so many, which does not scorch the leaves? And sometimes, when a traveller lies down here to sleep the siesta, he hears sounds of footsteps coming and going, and noises of dogs and fowls, and of children shouting and laughing, and voices of people talking. But when he starts up and listens, the sounds grow faint, and seem at last to pass away into the tree with a low murmur as of wind among the leaves.

The story of this haunted tree is one to be read out of doors—under English trees, let us say, that reflect by their likeness in unlikeness the great trunk of the tropical Ombú. No story that I know, written in our time, so conveys the desire of life, and the extremest cruelty of death, without once breaking the taleteller's profound pleasure in the things he has to relate. In *Green Mansions* too, it may be remembered, the daughter of the Di-di meets her fate in a tree; and that story can be read along with *El Ombú* and the later English tale *An Old Thorn*, which form a trilogy without a parallel in English fiction.

More about the Ombú tree is to be learnt from *Far Away and Long Ago*:

The house where I was born was named *Los Veinte-cinco Ombúes*, that is the "Twenty-five Ombú Trees." For there were in fact just so many of them in a long row. It is a tree of huge girth, and yet the wood is soft and spongy, unfit for firewood and otherwise useless, and the leaves are poisonous. Being of so little service to man it is likely to die out: but it formed a gigantic landmark on those South American plains and gave welcome shade to man and horse from the sun.

On the Pampas or on the Downs, we find how important a rôle is that of the single figure in the foreground. A tree, a shepherd, a beggar-on-horseback, a hermit like "Con-Stair Lovair," a patriarch like Don Evaristo Penalva serves to focus to a fine degree the particular spot of earth that is described. On the South Downs, it may be a picture of a farm-boy, "The Boy with the Thistle":

> He wore a round grey peakless cap, and for ornament he had fastened in the middle of it, where there had perhaps once been a top-knot or ball, a big woolly thistle-flower.

No doubt there are dangers in this kind of figurative particularity. Some people who attempt it become too diffuse in their wish to be exact, and end by growing garrulous over a bit of straw or a stray pig. Again, a wrong word or a touch of self-consciousness is fatal as the cough of the hunter who hopes to pass for a stone or a tree-trunk when stalking a deer. The naturalist in Hudson saves him at the point where you may think him getting too notionable for his woodcraft. Indeed it is the reaction between nature and human nature in his work which makes it interesting. The insect race and the bird race and the human race—are they not alike alive, alike confounded by the mortal decay of things? In the September pages of his Sussex book, he described "the wind sweeping through the yellow bennets with a long scythe-like sound." Then the thought of the past summer's insect life, and the noise of all those fine small voices blending into one voice, and the glistening of their minute swift-moving bodies like thin dark lines on the air, overtakes him:

And now in so short a time, in a single day and night as it seems, it is all over, the feast and fairy dance of life; the myriads of shining gem-like bodies turned to dead dust, the countless multitudes of brilliant little individual souls dissipated into thin air, and blown whithersoever the wind blows.

It may seem that the impression this leaves is too mournful, but though a tinge of melancholy—even, it may be, of ingrained melancholy—does show in these pages, the whole sense of the spectacle of life which they bear is a large and invigorative one.

Take the sketch of Shepherd Caleb Bawcombe's mother and the black sheep-dog, Jack. The dog was of the old Welsh type once common in Wiltshire, and a great adder-killer: "I can see her now," said Caleb, "sitting on that furze bush, in her smock and leggings, with a big hat like a man's on her head—for that's how she dressed." But presently she jumped up crying out that she felt a snake under her, and snatched off the shawl on which she had been sitting. There, sure enough, appeared the head of an adder: and Jack dashed at the bush, seized the snake and killed it.

A RARE TRAVELLER

Take again the "History of Tommy Ierat," in the same book. The long life and curiously easy death of this man, as there told, are affecting as the end of Sir Launcelot in the *Morte d'Arthur*. One can hardly say more than that.

In the last chapter of his autobiography, by turning the glass upon himself he shows where his boyish hopes and fears were leading him, when his own story was but a quarter told, with the years of his full experience still to come:

. . . Barring accidents, I could count on thirty, forty, even fifty years, with their summers and autumns and winters. And that was the life I desired . . . the life the heart can conceive—*the earth life*.

Of that life so conceived he was the natural historian, and it is worth note that, when other tests fail, he got his effect by looking into the most curious of all natural phenomena—himself. For Nature, the arch-revealer, when she finds a man to her mind, can make him a part of her own expression. *Idle Days in Patagonia*—a book in which the professional naturalist seems at times struggling with the natural man—serves to show how it came about. There, as he describes the bird-sounds, and the resonant quality of their notes, which tells you of the mysterious bell, "somewhere in the air, suspended on nothing," or, as he recalls the Plains, and the grey waste, he has already let you far into his secret.

He speaks of the state of mind, induced by the

change of consciousness, that comes to a man who has been long in a state of solitude. It leads, he says, to "a revelation of an unfamiliar and unsuspected nature" hidden under the nature we commonly recognise; and it is accounted for by a sudden awakening in us of the old primitive animal instinct which is often accompanied (as it is in the very young) by an intense delight. To that delight, instinctive yet spiritual in its higher development, he returns in the portrait he draws of his mother:

> Everything beautiful in sight or sound, that affected me, came associated with her, and this was especially so with flowers. Her feeling for them was little short of adoration. To her they were little voiceless messengers from heaven, symbols of a place and a beauty beyond our power to imagine. Her favourites were mostly among wild flowers that are never seen in England. But [he says] if ever I should return to the Pampas I should go out in search of them, and seeing them again, feel that I was communing with her spirit.

This is a confession which explains something of the faculty that must be possessed by one who is more than a mere chronicler of wild life—the curious power which can see earth transformed by sympathetic understanding. The delight he found in that life did not fail as time went; it grew instead, and gained a deeper purchase upon his mind. And even when he was shut out from Nature in London for long periods, sick and poor and friendless, it was his sure consolation.

A RARE TRAVELLER

One wayfaring book of his remains to be described—*Afoot in England*. It appeared more than ten years ago, but I only chanced upon it after reading the later English books. Some chapters and pages of it are in his most characteristic vein; and they help one to find the measure of his traveller's philosophy. It has an introduction on Guide Books well worth pondering. He goes to a Guide Book town, much boomed, made notorious by railway placards; and even there he comes upon a peal of bells which recalls the Monk of Eynsham's Easter Bells—" a ringing of marvellous sweetness as if all the bells in the world, or whatsoever is of sounding, had been rung together at once." He travels in Cobbett's footsteps to Coombe and " Uphusband " or Hurstbourne Tarrant; he goes to Salisbury, Stonehenge, Bath, and Wells. He considers cathedrals anew as bird resorts. At Salisbury he finds a wondrous population of birds: swallows, martins, swifts; to say nothing of daws, starlings and sparrows: even kestrels, and stock-doves, instead of the common town pigeons, are of that church-keeping company:

Nor could birds in all this land find a more beautiful building to rest on—unless I except Wells Cathedral, solely on account of its west front, beloved of daws, where their numerous black company have so fine an appearance. Salisbury, so vast in size, is yet a marvel of beauty in its entirety. Still to me the sight of the birds' airy gambols and the sound of their voices, from the deep human-like dove tones to the perpetual subdued rippling running-water sound of the aerial martins, must always be a principal element in the beautiful effect. Nor do I know a building where Nature has done more in enhancing the loveliness of man's work with her added colouring. . . . This colouring is most beautiful [he adds] on a day of flying clouds and a blue sky with a brilliant sunshine on the vast building after a shower.

A cathedral to him, as to Ibañez, is a cathedral and something more. It is part of the indigenous growth of the country, and, in exploring it, he is like St. Brandan in *The Golden Legend* discovering an Isle of Birds.

A discoverer of strange things in familiar places, Hudson saw birds as another race, not so far from our own, a little more aerial, a little less earthy. At another remove, the insect race is again behind, or a little below the bird race. The lowest of all, I am afraid, is of the homunculus type—one which invariably moves his spleen. For we must admit that he is splenetic at times. He is angry with the Toby Philpots of Chichester; he is annoyed with Cornish folk—I imagine because they are not like the Devon folk he loves so well. He is angry with fashionable women who go to Holy Communion with aigrettes in their hats. He is annoyed by dirty little boys who follow their instincts, and stone or catch little birds. But this is only because he is a kindhearted vagabond who is ready to love all creatures that on earth do dwell, so long as they are not too degenerate to preserve their natural instincts. He is one among the rare itinerants who have revealed the beauty of this country by their affectionate art—including White of Selborne, Old Crome, Constable, Turner, Richard Jefferies, Wordsworth, and certain unnamed and undistinguished provincial poets. There are pages of his that enshrine scenes and memories of places to be ranked with Old Crome's "Mousehold Heath," the picture of Appin sketched by Dorothy Wordsworth in her *Tour in Scotland*, Dyer's *Grongar Hill*, Bewick's thumb-nail vignettes of Prudhoe-on-Tyne, and Constable's "Old Sarum."

In days to come, when nearly all the wildness of Britain is tamed, men will look back with envy to Hudson's account of the birds in Savernake, and of the London daws, now growing scarcer every year, that rose to fly with the homing crows as they passed over Kensington Gardens.

Of two more books which are part of his English cycle, the first is *Birds in Town and Village*, which has a greenfinch interlude for the consolation of true bird-lovers, a charming tale of a duet between a girl and a nightingale, and many other characteristic vagabond passages. What will surprise some readers, less tolerant than the naturalist himself, is a critical appreciation of a concert of London sparrows. The fit sequel to that is the chapter on "Chanticleer"; and there are other London contributions and notably one on the moorhens in Hyde Park. The book is illustrated by some wonderfully brilliant bird-portraits by E. J. Detmold—brilliantly coloured and sunlit. Indeed

ERNEST RHYS

the blue-tit and goldfinch, in one picture, are almost dazzling—every wing-feather detailed like a fan.

The other is *The Book of a Naturalist*, which adds some delightful pages, natural and human-natural, to the writer's account of Britain rediscovered. It opens with a pine wood, and it ends with earthworms and an experiment with acacia-leaves to test the value of the worm as a lawn-maker. Two chapters on the mole, two on the heron considered as an ancient British notable and aristocrat, and four on serpents, native and foreign, serve to carry on the record. The story of the she-rat that communed with her natural enemy, a cat, and in the end tried to steal the fluff from the cat's abundant side-whiskers, and so provoked a misunderstanding, is an unexpected diversion, since Hudson was not fond of rats, and has even been known to call them those "cursèd cattle." But the book is above all to be gratefully remembered for its scenes and episodes of the wild chronicle of the English shires:—an enchanting June evening in the Valley of the Wiltshire Avon, when the ghost-moths were out upon their love-dance over the dusky meadows; an adder episode in the New Forest, when the creature proved to have an under surface of the most exquisite turquoise blue; or a brown-purple field of fritillaries, or ginny-flowers, which are of the wild lily kind, pendulous as a harebell, and of a delicate pink chequered with dark maroon-purple.

These voyages and discoveries seemed to occur

A RARE TRAVELLER

to Hudson so easily, that they leave one newly penetrated with the sense of the wild splendour, the beauty inexhaustible, of the new-old country that he travelled. No need for him to go back to Guayana, since he found his tropics in a Wiltshire meadow, and his wood beyond the world in Hants or Dorset. There are many wild places—downs, woods and lowlands, that will miss hereafter that tall, grey, falcon-faced traveller.

PRINTED BY
THE TEMPLE PRESS AT LETCHWORTH
IN GREAT BRITAIN

Printed in July 2019
by Rotomail Italia S.p.A., Vignate (MI) - Italy